UNDERSTANDING AND LOVING A PERSON WITH

DEPRESSION

*Biblical and Practical Wisdom
to Build Empathy, Preserve Boundaries,
and Show Compassion*

STEPHEN ARTERBURN, M.Ed.
AND BRENDA HUNTER, Ph.D.

David C Cook®

transforming lives together

UNDERSTANDING AND LOVING A PERSON WITH DEPRESSION
Published by David C Cook
4050 Lee Vance Drive
Colorado Springs, CO 80918 U.S.A.

Integrity Music Limited, a Division of David C Cook
Brighton, East Sussex BN1 2RE, England

The graphic circle C logo is a registered trademark of David C Cook.

The website addresses recommended throughout this book are offered as a
resource to you. These websites are not intended in any way to be or imply an
endorsement on the part of David C Cook, nor do we vouch for their content.

Details in some stories have been changed to protect the identities of the persons involved.

Unless otherwise noted, all Scripture quotations are taken from the Holy Bible,
NEW INTERNATIONAL VERSION®, NIV®. Copyright © 1973, 2011 by Biblica,
Inc.® Used by permission. All rights reserved worldwide. NEW INTERNATIONAL
VERSION® and NIV® are registered trademarks of Biblica, Inc. Use of either trade-
mark for the offering of goods or services requires the prior written consent of
Biblica, Inc. Scripture quotations marked ESV are taken from the ESV® Bible
(The Holy Bible, English Standard Version®), copyright © 2001 by Crossway,
a publishing ministry of Good News Publishers. Used by permission. All rights
reserved; NLT are taken from the Holy Bible, New Living Translation, copyright
© 1996, 2007 by Tyndale House Foundation. Used by permission of Tyndale
House Publishers, Inc., Carol Stream, Illinois 60188. All rights reserved.

Library of Congress Control Number 2017935676
ISBN 978-1-4347-1054-3
eISBN 978-1-4347-1236-3

The Author is represented by and this book is published in association with the
literary agency of WordServe Literary Group, Ltd., www.wordserveliterary.com.

Cover Design: Amy Konyndyk
Cover Photo: Getty Images

Printed in the United States of America
First Edition 2017

6 7 8 9 10 11 12 13 14 15

050521

I wish to dedicate this book to my husband, Don ...
a faithful, committed, and stalwart man

Contents

Introduction

I'm so glad you've chosen this book on depression from the Arterburn Wellness Series. The series is designed for you, the person who has a loved one or friend who is perhaps facing the lowest point of his or her life. While this book has been written for you, the caregiver, there's valuable information for the depressed person in your life as well.

Before I introduce you to Brenda Hunter, the writer of this book, I want to share my own brushes with depression. As the radio host for *New Life Live*, a one-hour call-in show that is on every day, I've talked to literally thousands of callers who were either in the middle of depression themselves or trying to help a loved one.

Depression is a very real malady. I should know; I've been there.

In my family's West Texas culture, we did not go to see counselors. You took care of problems inside of your fence. As I look back on it now, it was like we felt we needed to lie or deny the reality of our struggles if it would make Jesus look better. Growing up like that, I shared very little of what troubled me, and I lived feeling isolated and detached from nearly everyone around me. At age eighteen, I had some very painful, ungrieved, and unresolved losses from a heartbreaking experience, one like I've never experienced since. I was struggling to survive and had no idea the shame-filled way of life was a result of not dealing with my depression.

When I went to see a physician at Baylor University Hospital, I thought I should simply get a B-12 shot like my mother had taken—something that could give me some energy. After talking with me for a few minutes (without my taking off my sunglasses), the doctor told me she believed I was depressed. She asked if I was safe, and, of course, I told her I was.

But I was not.

I wanted to die, and if I had had access to pills, I would have taken them. I knew that would have stopped my pain. Violent ways of ending it all weren't for me ... I was too afraid of blood.

I found out later that suicide sometimes runs deep in a family tree. Sadly, when it is in *your* family, it becomes more of a tangible option than if no one has tried or succeeded.

Suicide had happened in my family.

My grandfather was treated for depression with electroconvulsive therapy (ECT) long before people were sedated prior to going through it (as they are now, though it is used infrequently). It helped him for a while, but he vowed he would never go back to that facility in Dallas and experience the horror of ECT. When the depression sank back in, he lived up to his words. He ended his life at the barrel of a gun. My mother found him in the garage under the car. In the wake of his death, he left our family and small church congregation confused, broken, humiliated, and full of shame. I didn't find out about what had really happened to my grandfather until I was a senior in high school.

Knowing the story of my grandfather's despair did not cause me to realize I was suffocating in my own depression. And I didn't know I should seek help for it. The physician at the Baylor Clinic saw that I was depressed and put me on an old antidepressant named Elavil. I took it, felt numb, and gained about thirty pounds. That is what the medication did back then. Fortunately, there are more effective medications without a weight-gaining side effect. I hated that medication, but it likely saved my life.

There would be two other times in the future when fighting depression would be my most important battle. I survived all three acute episodes, but not by much.

Like many other depressed strugglers, I did not really want to die. I just wanted the pain to go away. And I wanted the world and all the people to go with it. It was a dark and dismal misery that I suffered alone and in isolation. Those who loved me and those who lived with me didn't understand what I was going through. Their trite suggestions, superficial scripture quoting, and the sometimes spiritual arrogance seeping out of their pores truly made matters worse. Whatever shame I was carrying before the depression, and the shame of being depressed and not able to pull myself up by my bootstraps, only deepened my depression and feelings of isolation.

Most of these people cared for and truly loved me. They just didn't know what to say or do. I think back on my own life, the people I tried to help early on as a social worker, and I realize that I really had about half a clue as to what to say or do to help them. To people whom I genuinely loved, I offered superficial and unhelpful words instead of giving them what they needed: compassionate wisdom (not blundering platitudes). Like so many of us, I felt the need to say something when it would have been best to just be present without any failed attempts at being helpful.

If you are living with and loving someone with depression, you may have said a thousand inadequate words. Perhaps you are still feeling a myriad of negative emotions like anger, frustration, hopelessness, and despair. You are not alone. It is much more common to be ill-equipped in the face of depression than to be adequately prepared to understand, express appropriate compassion, and even be able to utter something that might help. That is the reason for this series, and especially this one on depression.

It is my desire that when you finish this book, it will have at least three results:

First, I hope you will have a deeper understanding of the condition of depression and the different ways it manifests itself.

Second, I hope you better understand the person you love and or live with at every stage of recovery or setback in progress.

Third, I hope you discover what is the most healing path for yourself and how you can help the depressed person you love without being enmeshed by his or her condition.

Depression does not have to be synonymous with destruction or detachment. You can love and live with someone who is depressed without having it destroy your own life or detach you from the person. You can be both healthy and helpful if you will implement the principles presented here. I hope this book will give you many of the answers—and a large portion of hope—you have been looking for.

Though I'm not the main author for this book or any of the books in the Arterburn Wellness Series, the authors have been carefully chosen for their knowledge, skills, experience, and compassion for the topics they're writing about. Dr. Brenda Hunter, a psychologist and licensed professional counselor, has faced her own bouts with depression, but today she counsels hundreds of people every year—both the depressed and those, like you, who love them. This is really a fantastic book that will help do what the title says it will do: Understand and Love.

—Stephen Arterburn

Preface

Depression has risen to epidemic levels in the United States. According to the National Institutes of Mental Health (NIMH), in any given year, 9.5 percent of the population, or approximately 9.5 million adults, suffer from a depressive illness.[1] In the spring of 2016, the Centers for Disease Control and Prevention (CDC) released data suggesting that suicide rates in the United States are higher than they were in 1999.[2] Why this sad upsurge in depression? We could blame stress, the sluggish economy, world instability, or terrorism in our own backyards.

While all these factors play a role in explaining the depression epidemic, are there other reasons for the darkness and hopelessness the depressed feel? In his book *Tribe*, Sebastian Junger suggests that American society—with all its human disconnects—is to blame. For example, parents are not as emotionally close to their kids as they need to be, kids spend too much time on their smartphones, neighbors only speak on occasion, young adults suffer from too many breakups, and most of us aren't deeply rooted in the places where we live. Moreover, community—a real sense of life together—is woefully lacking.

These are just some of the themes we will explore in this book to expand our understanding of the mental illness that is depression. Let me be clear at this point: this book is intended to help you understand depression's complexities. It is not a book about blaming yourself or others for this debilitating illness. Instead, it is about growing in awareness and learning new skills.

While numerous books have been written about depression—including the excellent personal account by writer William Styron entitled *Darkness Visible: A Memoir of Madness,* in which he chronicles his descent into severe clinical depression—few books have been written to help the depressed person's tribe: his spouse, parent, friend, coworker, or child. When someone you love struggles with depression, it can be taxing beyond measure. You must deal with all the depressive's negativity, low self-esteem, hopelessness, and irritability on a daily basis. You may feel angry, frustrated, helpless, and somewhat depressed yourself. And if the depressive is an adult child, he may blame you for his angst, and in your sixties or even seventies, you may find yourself carrying this burden. As a friend of mine in her nineties said, "The golden years aren't so golden. When we are having health problems and our strength is waning, we often see an adult child struggle or even mess up his life and watch our grandchildren suffer." Moreover, if the person you love is severely depressed or suffers from a major depressive disorder, you may be afraid she will become so trapped in black hopelessness that suicide becomes a possibility. Not only can this be paralyzing for you, but it can rob you of any joy in the relationship. You may even feel at times that it sucks the life out of you.

Take heart. In this book, I will walk alongside you as one who has spent years working as a psychologist and licensed professional counselor with depressed and anxious clients in a clinical setting. In addition, I want to share my firsthand experience of sinking into depression and my spouse's solicitude in helping me come out of it. A psychiatrist and coworker of mine once said, "We can't take someone to a place we have never been." I who have experienced depression firsthand can tell you just what life looks like from that place of darkness; I can also inform you of what works in coming out of depression to a sunnier place. Moreover, I watched my optimistic husband sink into depression when he suffered a major concussion and took a drug that induced depression. Basically, I have lived through both sides of the depressive experience and can speak from both perspectives.

The road isn't easy for the depressed person or those who love him. Sometimes, the journey is long. But as long as you keep hope alive, it is possible to learn how to defeat negative thinking and find healing for those ancient inner wounds. Know that you are not alone. Many of the people around you have a friend, spouse, or child struggling with depression. So let's walk through this together.

In these pages, I have used the word *depressive* to describe the loved one who has the mood disorder (because it is shorter than "your depressed loved one"). Also, even though more women than men get depressed, I have alternated gender pronouns. As a former English teacher, I simply cannot use a plural pronoun such as "their" to refer back to a singular person. Finally, the stories mentioned are accounts from friends, recent interviews granted with permission, or composites of exchanges with numerous clients over many years. In one instance, I have shared a beautiful story of forgiveness with the client's consent. In all instances, names, professions, and locales have been changed. I have, except in one instance where the client has given permission, made every effort to protect confidentiality.

It is my hope that this book will not only help you understand the depressed person in your life but also deepen your compassion and empathy and that this understanding will bring healing in its wings. At the same time, I will encourage you to set healthy boundaries and engage in self-care. It is essential that you don't get lost in the world of depression, that you maintain good physical and mental health, and that you retain some measure of control over your life. As the stewardess always says before a flight, "Put your oxygen mask on first before helping others"—a message that definitely applies when dealing with someone you love who is depressed. In addition, I want to offer you hope: depression can be treated effectively and people can recover. All of us, no matter how severe our trials, need to hold onto hope and never let go. I will show you how. Read on.

Brenda Hunter, Ph.D.
Chapel Hill, North Carolina

CHAPTER ONE

"A Cage without a Key"

Depression is the inability to construct a future.

Rollo May, *Love and Will*

That is the thing about depression: a human being can survive almost anything as long as she sees the end in sight. But depression is so insidious, and it compounds daily, that it is impossible to ever see the end. The fog is like a cage without a key.

Elizabeth Wurtzel, *Prozac Nation*

Janet came into my office complaining of anxiety and mild depression. She began to tell me about her difficult marriage to a man who was living with chronic pain. Not only did she feel helpless because she was unable to understand what he was experiencing, but communication had been a problem since the genesis of their seven-year marriage: "We seldom talk about anything deep and meaningful. Most of our conversation is information sharing. Now my husband is in pain most of the time and is deeply depressed." I asked her to describe his behavior. She explained, "John is negative, irritable, and basically shut down. He won't talk about his feelings, his pain, or his worries. He pushes me away, and when I try to help him, he becomes downright hostile. I want to understand and help, I really do, but he is so negative it is nearly impossible."

Tom called me for couple's therapy—an unusual move, since most people who contact therapists are women. When I asked what prompted his call, he replied, "I'm worried about my wife. She has been depressed for several months, and, frankly, I don't know how to handle her. She often gets ticked off when I try to help her. She's irritable around our kids and cries a lot. She has lost weight and says she can't sleep. This woman who has a high-level job is having trouble with her colleagues at work. I think I'm getting depressed just being around her."

Sarah sat in my office and told me about her adolescent daughter. Looking worn and tired, she said, "Jan's grades have dropped from As to Cs, and she has become negative about her life. She says she has no friends and she hates school. There's a boy she's begun to hang out with—and he's not someone her father and I approve of. She used to be a pretty compliant kid, but now she argues with me about everything. Plus, she stays in her room with her door closed when she's home and listens to music or stares at her smartphone. I'm worried; I think she's depressed, and I don't know what to do."

Betsy came to small group, and at the end of the session, she wanted to talk about her best friend, Ann, who had retreated and was hard to reach by phone or email. She and Ann had become close friends several years earlier and had hit it off immediately. Both were single and hoped to marry. In addition, they had good jobs and close ties with their families. But when Ann ended a romantic relationship, she felt the loss keenly. Whenever the women got together, Ann talked incessantly about her tanked relationship, her low self-esteem, her insomnia, and her weight gain. When Betsy tried to help and offer advice, Ann shot her down.

Betsy said she could meet Ann feeling pretty good about life, but after thirty minutes in Ann's company, Betsy felt herself sinking like a boat with a hole in the bottom. And because she was also single, she had no one to go home to and share her frustration and confusion with. She wanted to know what she should do.

Do any of these accounts resonate with you? Let me just say at the outset that it's tough to have a depressive in your life, whether that person is a spouse, a child, a boss, a coworker, or a close friend. And if you find yourself frequently entering the dark atmosphere of someone who is depressed, someone who resists all your attempts to lift his mood and rejects all the advice you extend, you could find yourself feeling vulnerable and slowly sinking into negative thinking yourself.

If someone you love lapses into depression, it is important to understand just what depression involves and learn how to set healthy boundaries. You will need to take care of yourself while you try to show empathy and compassion for the depressive. Sometimes this is exquisitely hard to do.

June Cassidy found that when her husband, Frank, sank into a full-blown clinical depression after a heart attack and major setbacks at work, she felt distraught because she was unable to lift his mood. She was frustrated with him because all he did was go to work, come home, and throw himself on the bed. "This was the first time in thirty years of marriage that Frank had ever been depressed," June said. How did living with a depressed husband affect her? "I felt frustrated and helpless and found myself getting angrier and angrier." June said that since she had been depressed herself years earlier, she knew all about the self-loathing that accompanies depression, and she wondered if she could keep out of the pit of depression herself. She felt that her own mood was vulnerable. So she buried herself in work and encouraged her husband to see a psychiatrist. She also enlisted his good friends and golfing buddies to rally around him. June said those six months of dealing with her husband's depression were hard to bear. When Frank's depression finally lifted with the help of talk therapy, the antidepressant Lexapro, and lots of social support, her response was, "Praise be to God." Thankfully, Frank learned skills in therapy that have helped him avoid a recurrence.

There are multiple reasons someone lapses into depression. As we shall see in later chapters, genetic and environmental factors play critical roles in pushing an individual over the edge. Sometimes life is just too stressful. A person may have run as fast as she could for too long, and chronic stress—the kind that people learn to live with and therefore don't even recognize as stress—does her in. If she loses her job and cannot find another one in good time, she may find herself becoming severely depressed. In addition, I have treated men and women in their twenties and thirties who have lapsed into depression because of a heartrending breakup. They come to me in great angst because a romantic relationship went belly-up and they can't bear to be alone. They are worried because this is not the first time they have been unable to find lasting love.

Medical conditions and drugs can also sometimes cause a loved one to become depressed, as I learned firsthand when my husband, Don, became depressed after a severe head injury.

Don had always been an extrovert who was optimistic about life. A corporate lawyer for his entire career, Don felt the sun was always shining when he got up in the morning, no matter what the weather was like outside. He enjoyed making our coffee, and when he brought me a steaming cup of java as I was stretching and yawning, he was robust and cheerful. In our forty-two years of marriage, I had come to count on his stable mood and positive outlook on life.

But several years ago when he was running across the grass in flip-flops, Don fell. Fortunately, he did not hit his head, so I thought he was okay. But several days later when we were out for dinner, his mouth twisted into a ghoulish grimace. When I asked him what was going on, he told me that he had been having seizures in his left hand, left arm, and the left side of his mouth for days. "Why haven't you told me?" I asked anxiously. He said the seizures came and went, so he didn't believe they were serious. I insisted that we go to the ER immediately, and within hours, we learned that he had sustained a severe brain injury—a subdural hematoma, meaning that he had developed bleeding between the layers that surround the brain. With a subdural hematoma, the blood collects in the cranium and puts pressure on the brain, and if the pressure is great enough, death can ensue.

Although the doctors couldn't stop the bleeding, they put Don on drugs to prevent further seizures, and within days, his personality changed. My husband became gloomy, surly, and sometimes downright hostile. He, a man whose favorite word had been "productive," sat around for hours, slumped in his chair. I found it hard to get him to talk; basically, he was disinterested in life. He resented the fact that the doctor had told him not to drive for six months; he resented the fact that I had to chauffeur him everywhere.

I didn't know what to blame for the change in Don's personality—the injury, the heavy-duty antiseizure drugs he was taking, or both. But I was flummoxed by this new husband who had come to live in our house. I wanted to be empathic; after all, he had sustained a major concussion. But it was hard since he was so unhappy with life and with me. Oh, how I missed my former husband, my sunny companion of so many years. Would I ever get him back, or was this the "new normal"?

Despite the drugs he took daily, the bleeding in his skull refused to stop, creating pressure on his brain. Don was hospitalized at the University of North Carolina several times. It was a harrowing time in our marriage; one physician even told me to get ready to put him on life support.

Don fell in July, but by December, he was listing to one side as his cranium slowly filled with blood. When we went for a surgical consult, the neurosurgeon said he could perform a craniotomy—remove a section of Don's skull—to drain the blood, but "the brain wouldn't like it." He agreed to wait one more month to see if Don would improve. That was in early December. That month, my husband had the healing prayer team at our Anglican church lay hands on him, anoint him with oil, and pray their soothing, earnest prayers. Then something beautiful happened. When Don had his next CAT scan in January, it was evident the bleeding had finally stopped. Months later, Don's internist told him, "Don, I have other patients much younger than you who have had as severe a concussion as you, but none have come back like you have. You need to thank the man upstairs." We have. Multiple times. And we continue to do so.

The other good news? When Don was taken off the powerful drugs, my optimistic husband slowly returned.

I share this personal account with you to let you know I have been there and can understand firsthand some of your feelings in dealing with a loved one who is depressed. But I also want to encourage you to believe that the depressive in your life can begin to recover. Depression is a scary but treatable illness, but to receive that treatment, your depressed loved one will need to be diagnosed and treated for this mood disorder. Because severe depression is potentially fatal, it is imperative that the depressive see a psychiatrist for an evaluation. The doctor will then determine if medication is necessary. In addition, the depressive needs to engage in talk therapy to deal with his unresolved pain and better identify and eradicate his negative thinking.

As you explore the nature of depression and learn about ways to help your loved one deal with it, you are likely to get back that person you love—or even an improved version, since that spouse, friend, or child, through treatment, will have learned better ways to handle her life and manage her moods.

As an individual works with a trained therapist—exploring past traumas and difficult relationships, as well as his earliest attachments to parents—he grows in self-awareness. He is no longer a passive victim trapped in the darkness; he is more self-aware and has learned to combat automatic negative thinking and, hopefully, to forgive those who have wounded him. Clients say they learn to think about themselves and their situation in new and fresh ways. Using cognitive behavioral therapy, reality therapy, and interpersonal therapy, as well as biblical principles, I help clients with their negative thinking and help them process hurts and the subsequent anger caused by those wounds; I help them find their voices and make new choices. It's an arduous process, and it happens gradually over time.

When you love someone who is depressed, you need to be compassionate, supportive, and loving, because no matter how negative and resistant he seems, he depends on you greatly. You are his lifeline. A depressive feels unloved in his core, and he is well aware of the relationship difficulties in his life. He needs the stability your presence provides; he hungers for encouragement and hope, especially when he is fighting feelings of hopelessness. At the same time, you need to take care of yourself physically, emotionally, and spiritually. You need to set healthy boundaries and not allow the depressive's darkness to penetrate your soul. And if this is hard for you to do, think of it not as selfishness but as self-preservation. You may need to find a psychotherapist for yourself, particularly if you grew up in a home where boundaries were not observed—you may need to work on differentiating yourself from the depressive and strengthening your sense of self.

To move forward with the person in your life who is depressed, not only do you need to know his story—particularly his earliest attachments with his parents—but you need to understand the mental disorder that is depression. This understanding will help you become more empathic and, in the end, will help you *and* the depressive not only survive but thrive.

CHAPTER TWO

The Epidemic That Is Depression

We are living in an epidemic of depression. Every indicator
suggests that more people are depressed, more of the time, more
severely, and starting earlier in their lives than ever before.
Richard O'Connor, *Undoing Depression*

When J. K. Rowling finished her final Harry Potter book, she sank into a deep depression. She told NBC's Meredith Vieira that the first days were "terrible." Rowling said, "I was incredibly low. I was mourning the loss of this world that I had written about for so long and loved so much. I was also mourning the retreat it had been from ordinary life, which it had been."[1]

She began to ruminate about her adult life, remembering the death of her mother, the failure of her first marriage, and the births of her three children. It took her a week to deal with the loss of the magical world she had created. She said, "I didn't cry as I was writing, but when I finished writing, I had an enormous explosion of emotion, and I cried and cried and cried."[2]

This was not the first time Rowling had been depressed. She had moved to Portugal to teach English after the end of her first marriage, and it was there that she gave birth to her first daughter,

Jessica. She felt like a complete failure and like "all the color" had drained out of her life. She became fearful that her daughter would die: "I loved Jessica very, very much and was terrified something was going to happen to her. I'd gone into that very depressive mindset where everything has gone wrong so that this one good thing in my life will now go wrong as well."[3]

By her own admission, she was clinically depressed.

Writers have a propensity for getting depressed. Tennessee Williams, William Faulkner, Emily Dickinson, Sylvia Plath, Virginia Woolf, and Fyodor Dostoevsky all struggled with bouts of depression. Winston Churchill, Britain's prime minister twice and a recipient of the Nobel Prize in Literature, spoke of the "black dog of depression" that hounded him throughout his life. In his book *The Churchill Factor*, Boris Johnson says that Churchill "wrote more words than Dickens and Shakespeare combined" and kept "the black dog of depression at bay" with his painting, bricklaying, and prodigious output of words.[4] He laid two hundred bricks, wrote two thousand words, or painted most days during the years he was not prime minister. His mind was thus distracted from the painful feelings of worthlessness that depressives experience.

But other mortals get depressed as well. Tipper Gore, former wife of Al Gore, became clinically depressed when she was recovering from her son's nearly fatal car accident. She said, "It was definitely a clinical depression and one that I was going to have to have help to overcome. When you get to this point … you just can't will your way out of that or pray your way of out that or pull yourself up by the bootstraps out of that. You really have to go and get help, and I did. And I was treated for it successfully, I'm happy to report."[5]

In addition, a number of famous men in the Bible battled depression, from Job to the prophet Elijah to King David. In fact, numerous psalms chronicle David's feelings of loss, his abandonment by God, and his darkness of soul. Psalm 143 captures the fear, the sense of foreboding, the paralysis, and the hopelessness that often dog the depressive. David writes,

My enemy has chased me.
    He has knocked me to the ground
    and forces me to live in darkness like those in the grave.
I am losing all hope;
    I am paralyzed with fear. …

Come quickly, LORD, and answer me,
    for my depression deepens.
Don't turn away from me,
    or I will die.[6]

Another biblical character, the Old Testament prophet Jonah, became so angry and depressed after God showed compassion toward repentant Nineveh that he wanted to die. Perhaps you know the story: God ordered Jonah to leave his home and go to preach destruction and judgment on the people of Nineveh for all their evil deeds. Instead, Jonah, wishing to flee the presence of the Lord, got on a ship headed for Tarshish. However, the Lord sent a great storm, and Jonah told his men on board the ship to hurl him into the sea so the sea would stop raging. They did, and he was swallowed by a great fish. From the belly of the fish, he prayed, repented, and was thrown onto dry land so he could resume his journey to Nineveh. There, he finally delivered God's message; he told the people of Nineveh that their great city would be overthrown in forty days. They repented, just as he had feared; even the king covered himself with sackcloth and sat in ashes. Jonah became so furious that God had relented that he asked God to kill him, saying, "Therefore now, O LORD, please take my life from me, for it is better for me to die than live."[7]

Twice he asked God to kill him. Twice God responded, "Do you do well to be angry?"[8] God acknowledged what every psychotherapist knows: anger and hostility are often deeply embedded in a wish to die. But He also acknowledged that Jonah had a choice; he could choose whether or not to be angry. When he chose anger, God asked him if that was a good idea. This is something to ponder as we go deeper into the subject of depression.

Who Gets Depressed?

So who gets depressed? Perhaps your response will be "lots of us." All of us know someone who has battled depression, or maybe you have wrestled with the beast yourself at some time in your life.

Those of us who experience depression share common traits. Psychologist Richard O'Connor, Ph.D., who has struggled with depression himself, writes in his book *Undoing Depression* that people "with depression are good at being responsible. We are good soldiers, honest and industrious. We have high standards and are good at working autonomously."[9] He adds that depressed people work harder at living than anyone else, "although there is little payoff for our effort."[10]

According to a Stanford School of Medicine report, at least 10 percent of people in the United States will experience a major depressive disorder at some point in their lives, and twice as many women as men will suffer from this malady.[11] While everyone has blue days now and then, when someone experiences a major depressive disorder or a clinical depression, he has severe, disruptive symptoms that affect the way he feels and thinks, and these symptoms can last for weeks and months.

Types of Depression

Perhaps you feel you need to better understand the various types of depression in order to help the depressive in your life. I must warn you that the information I will give you is complex and may feel overwhelming at first. So buckle your seatbelt.

First, the fifth edition of the *Diagnostic and Statistical Manual*— or *DSM-5*—is the guidebook for those of us in the mental health profession. When someone comes into our offices with obvious symptoms of depression, not only do we do a diagnostic evaluation, but we check *DSM-5* to review the types of depression and their symptoms. According to *DSM-5*, "the common feature of all of these disorders is the presence of sad, empty or irritable mood, accompanied by somatic and cognitive changes that significantly affect the individual's ability to function."[12] The following sections describe the depressive disorders as classified by *DSM-5*.

Major Depressive Disorder

When someone has a major depressive disorder, she experiences severe symptoms that interfere with her ability to function at work, to sleep, to eat, and to enjoy relationships. The feelings of sadness are intense and pervasive. She may have a single episode of major depressive disorder or recurrent episodes that vary from mild to moderate to severe. To be given this diagnosis, an individual must have five or more of the following symptoms during the same two-week period:

- depressed mood most of the day and nearly every day
- diminished interest or pleasure in all or almost all activities every day
- either significant weight loss or weight gain
- insomnia or excessive daytime sleepiness
- observable agitation or slowing down of physical movements
- fatigue or loss of energy daily
- feelings of worthlessness or inappropriate guilt nearly every day
- diminished ability to think or concentrate (brain fog) and indecisiveness nearly every day
- recurrent thoughts of death or suicide, a suicidal attempt, or a specific plan to commit suicide[13]

Persistent Depressive Disorder

Formerly called dysthymia, persistent depressive disorder is characterized by a depressed mood that has lasted for at least two years (or at least one year in children and adolescents). Persistent depressive disorder often starts in childhood, adolescence, or early adulthood. Sometimes, individuals have experienced parental loss.

Often, a patient will say, "I have felt this way for as long as I can remember."[14] A person with this diagnosis may also have had episodes of major depression preceding or during this period marked by dysthymic disorder. He must have two or more of the following symptoms:

- poor appetite or overeating
- insomnia or hypersomnia (sleeps too much)
- low energy or fatigue
- low self-esteem
- poor concentration or indecisiveness
- feelings of hopelessness[15]

Disruptive Mood Dysregulation Disorder

Disruptive mood dysregulation disorder is a new diagnostic category pertaining to children, and it describes children who have been persistently irritable nearly every day or nearly every other day for twelve or more months. To receive this diagnosis, a child must have severe temper outbursts that occur three or more times a week, and these outbursts must be developmentally inappropriate. This behavior needs to occur before age ten, and the diagnosis cannot be given prior to age six.[16]

Premenstrual Dysphoric Disorder

Many women will celebrate the addition of premenstrual dysphoric disorder to the *DSM*'s list of depressive disorders because it validates their experiences. Women who suffer from this disorder have marked mood swings, increased irritability, feelings of hopelessness, and self-deprecating thoughts during the final week before their periods. In addition, they must exhibit at least one of the following symptoms: diminished interest in their usual activities, difficulty concentrating, lack of energy, change in appetite, insomnia or sleeping too much, and feeling overwhelmed or experiencing physical symptoms such as breast tenderness.[17] These symptoms begin to abate once their periods start.

Substance/Medication-Induced Depressive Disorder

Substance/medication-induced depressive disorder is caused by substances such as alcohol or cocaine or medications such as psychotropic drugs. In other words, depressive symptoms are produced while the person is using the substance and usually abate once the substance is discontinued.[18]

Why We Get Depressed

We get depressed for a variety of reasons. We may become depressed in adulthood when we develop a serious illness, lose a job and can't pay the bills, have an unhappy marriage, or get divorced. In adolescence, we may have to deal with parental loss, rejection by peers, too much homework, and sleep deprivation, among other things.

The majority of cancer patients experience mild to moderate depression when they are first given their diagnosis. Chronic pain that is relentlessly present day and night can also lead to depression. Clients have said that dealing with chronic pain exhausts them and not knowing whether it will ever end makes them feel depressed and even crazy. Sadly, depression makes chronic pain worse.

Sometimes we get depressed when we have lived with chronic stress for far too long, and it leaves us feeling empty inside. We may have neglected our well-being for years and thrown regular sleep and a nourishing diet to the winds. The workaholic who drives his body relentlessly for months or years may find that he has become deeply depressed without understanding why. As a psychotherapist, I have seen a number of clients, mostly single women, who live for their work and neglect other areas of their lives, like play, health, nutritious food, sleep, and meaningful relationships.

We live unbalanced lives at our peril because they produce chronic stress, which often leads to depression, and depression is associated with life-threatening illnesses. I have worked with cancer patients who, prior to their diagnosis, felt as if they were on a treadmill and couldn't get off, or rats were nibbling them to death, or they were caged birds. In therapy, these clients learn that their driven nature started in childhood when they were loved not for who they were but for their stellar performances. They examine their core beliefs and work to "change the soup," or generate a new and improved lifestyle in order to get well. They also examine core beliefs that operate out of sight, out of mind but greatly influence their self-esteem and their intimate relationships.

In addition, unhappy marriages can be perilous for women. As women, we feel the emotional distance in our marriages keenly and are unable to compartmentalize like men do after a fight or a nasty argument. It is not surprising that researchers have found a link between heart disease and marital discord. As women, we are relational from birth and need the love and support of our husbands to achieve our best selves. The inability to resolve conflicts with a spouse or establish appropriate boundaries with others, particularly family members, can be a breeding ground for depression in women.

Others of us get depressed when we find ourselves isolated, lonely, and without sufficient friends or connections, such as when mothers stay at home with small children. As I said to one mom who came for therapy when she was home alone with a one-year-old and a three-year-old child and no social support, "Show me a woman who has been home alone with small children for a week, and I will show you a woman who's soon to be depressed." As I wrote in my book *In the Company of Women*, women need other women from the cradle to the grave. Isolation and loneliness inevitably take us down and keep us from feeling fulfilled in our lives.

Families and Depression

Does depression run in families? Sometimes it appears so: look at the Hemingway family. Nobel laureate Ernest Hemingway, who committed suicide in 1961, lost his father, Clarence, to suicide. Two of his siblings also took their own lives, as did his granddaughter Margaux, who died of a drug overdose. Some of us can trace depression backward, generation after generation, remembering when a grandmother took to her bed in her fifties for a time, when a parent had a breakdown and was hospitalized for severe depression, or when a grandparent committed suicide.

That leads us to this question: Do our genes predispose us to depression? Scientists who have looked at "heritability" (the percentage of the cause of the illness due to genes) in identical twins have found that about 40 to 50 percent of major depression is due to genetic factors. This means that in severe depression, 50 percent of the cause is genetic and 50 percent is the result of environmental causes.[19] As of yet, no single depression gene has been identified, and some scientists believe that multiple genetic factors work together with environmental factors to produce depression.[20]

Environmental Factors

What are these environmental factors? If a person grows up and experiences neglect or physical or sexual abuse, she may suffer from a clinical depression in adulthood. Often a grown man is not aware that the single parent who came home late night after night—leaving a twenty-dollar bill on the table for him, a young middle schooler, to order pizza—was neglectful. He knows he sometimes had to cook his own meals, iron his own clothes, clean the house, and spend some weekends alone. But he never allows himself to feel the full import of the parental neglect—that is, until he sinks into a deep depression in adulthood, believing that no one cares for his soul.

And the woman who fended off her drunken father in the bedroom night after night, pretending to be asleep, who left home at seventeen and had a baby out of wedlock at eighteen, may never process her father's sexual abuse until she becomes seriously depressed. One study looked specifically at sexual abuse of women and men in childhood and its relationship to adult-onset depression. It found that while girls were more often abused than boys, this devastating and stressful early life experience affected both sexes physiologically and predisposed them to adult depression.[21]

Also, if a person grew up in a household where Mom or Dad was depressed, not only did he suffer because of his parent's irritability and emotional unavailability, but he may have learned deficient coping skills just by watching his depressed parent handle life. As a colleague of mine said, "If Mom couldn't get out of bed in the morning, we may not think it odd when we become depressed as adults and want to stay in bed, turning our faces to the wall." As children, all of us learned habits and ways of dealing with life's challenges from our parents, and some who suffer from major depression look back on painful childhoods they may never have examined or worked through.

Loss and Depression

Finally, loss in childhood may be a powerful harbinger of depression. When a child loses a parent early in life, she may be more vulnerable to depression later on. In his classic book *Loss: Sadness and Depression*, John Bowlby, the late British psychoanalyst, wrote that the depressive is more likely than others to have lost a parent in childhood and will have experienced feelings of powerlessness and "impotence as a consequence."[22]

William Styron, author of *Lie Down in Darkness* and *Sophie's Choice*, felt that the death of his mother was the genesis of his later depression. In *Darkness Visible: A Memoir of Madness*, he writes that "loss in all of its manifestations is the touchstone of depression—in the progress of the disease and, most likely, in its origin."[23] Not only was his father deeply depressed when Styron was growing up, but Styron lost his mother when he was a vulnerable thirteen-year-old boy embarking on adolescence. He felt he was not allowed to grieve her death at the time and that this was part of the reason he sank into depression later in life. He described his mother's death as traumatic and said it created "nearly inexplicable emotional havoc."[24]

To experience parental loss in childhood or early adolescence is to be deprived of economic stability, a safe harbor, and a source of protection and love, as well as a wealth of important childhood experiences. I lost my father early in life and did not realize the magnitude of what I had lost until midlife. Only recently have I processed the full import of losing my father in early childhood. This is what I wrote:

I stood on the bank of the Oconaluftee River several summers ago, at the foot of the dam, staring at the place where my young father had lost his life when I was a mere two-year-old. I had finally come to the place I had avoided all my life.

The story of my father's death happened this way: He and my mother, along with my baby sister, Sandy, had moved to a house near the Oconaluftee River in Bryson City, North Carolina. At the end of that hot moving day, he and a doctor's eight-year-old son decided to go swimming in the ice-cold waters of the dam. Within minutes, he was struggling and grabbed the boy's arm, pulling him under. The boy broke free and ran to the house, where two Cherokee Indian girls were helping my mother move in. One ran to the edge of the water and dove in, searching for my father's body while my mother waited anxiously on shore. When his body was finally retrieved, my father, an excellent swimmer, was long dead. A cardiologist at Duke said years later that my twenty-five-year-old father had had a heart attack.

How did my father's death affect me? First, it stripped our little family of any significant financial provision and meant that I grew up below the poverty line. Although Mother worked full time as a telephone operator, we were precariously poor. It also meant that I was raised by my less-functional parent. My father had gone to North Carolina State University and had worked as a county agent, while Mother had not finished high school. He came from a loving, intact family; she had lost her mother at age five and had been raised by a stepmother and her alcoholic father. She yearned for the mother she had lost all her life, and her losses made her prone to depression.

It was in the stacks of Lauinger Library at Georgetown University, while I was working on my doctorate in psychology, that I began to mourn the death of my young father and become aware of the roots of my depressive feelings. It matters if one loses a parent in childhood. It matters greatly if a parent was an alcoholic or an abusive or absent parent.

What, you might ask, about parental loss through divorce? That, too, can be devastating to a child, particularly if the parent who leaves home sees the child seldom. This loss, experienced as abandonment, becomes coupled with rejection when visits are few. Sometimes the child believes that Mom or Dad did not love him enough to stay, and he internalizes feelings of blame or false guilt for their divorce.

Some women and men are so scarred by parental divorce that they hesitate to marry; deep down, they are afraid that they too will experience divorce. Others doubt that they will ever be worthy of love or enjoy lasting, committed love; as a consequence, they may battle depression in adulthood. When adult children of divorce come for therapy, I suggest they read a compelling book entitled *The Unexpected Legacy of Divorce: The 25 Year Landmark Study* by Judith S. Wallerstein, Julia M. Lewis, and Sandra Blakeslee. In this study of children of divorce, the authors interviewed the children when they were young; then the researchers returned twenty-five years later to see how the children—now adults—were faring. They found that many of these young adults were in great psychological pain. Some believed their romantic relationships would falter and fail, just like their parents' marriages had done. While this is a difficult book for adult children of divorce to read, it lets them know they are not alone and validates their feelings and concerns about intimate relationships.

I also recommend this book for couples who are considering divorce. I have found that some pull back from the brink and begin to work on their marriages in earnest after reading *The Unexpected Legacy of Divorce*. They say they love their young children too much to consign them to such grief and pain.

Suicide

What makes depression so troubling is the possibility that the depressive may decide that life is not worth living. According to *DSM-5*, suicide is a possibility *at all times* during a major depressive episode. Risk factors include having a past history of suicide threats or attempts, being male and single, and feeling hopeless.[25] Recent Centers for Disease Control and Prevention (CDC) data indicate that the number of suicides in the United States has risen significantly in recent years. In fact, suicide rates have gone up

24 percent since 1999, with the greatest increases among young girls and middle-age men. Girls ages ten to fourteen were the hardest hit, with a rise of 200 percent. As for men ages forty-five to sixty-four, the increase was 43 percent.[26]

Stop, I'm Overwhelmed

Perhaps at this point you feel overwhelmed with all you've learned so far about depression. When I told friends and clients I was writing a book about depression, they invariably asked if I could wade into this subject without getting depressed myself. I must admit I did have to take a day off periodically during those warm summer days when I was chained to my computer. Maybe you will need to take little breaks yourself. However, it is good to know what you are up against. Understanding the illness will help you deal with the one you love who is depressed with greater love and compassion, and it will help you take better care of yourself, both physically and emotionally.

I would encourage you to become a student of the depressive, especially if he or she is your spouse. Do you know this person's story? What was her early life like? Did he have a depressed parent when he was young and vulnerable? Was she ever physically, verbally, or sexually abused during the years she lived at home? Did he lose a parent to death or divorce? All of this matters. It matters greatly. As you learn more, you can become a better agent of healing.

Never lose hope or courage. Remember, it takes courage to live life cold sober. Far too many turn to substance abuse to deaden their pain. If you can deal with the depressive in your life with resilience, some optimism, and faith, you will emerge from this trial stronger and, ultimately, happier. I have seen remarkable courage in my clients, from terminal cancer patients to those with Lou Gehrig's disease (ALS) or chronic pain. It has enlarged my view of men and women to see such resilience and love for others in the face of overwhelming adversity.

And if you can, pray. Pray like you have never prayed before. Pray for the depressed person in your life, and pray for yourself—that you will have the strength and courage to make it through this demanding season of life. Prayer is powerful. God listens to our cries, and when we pray, we do not feel so helpless or alone. Why should we? We have the God of the universe on our side. And God doesn't just listen, He answers—sometimes in amazing ways.

CHAPTER THREE

When a Man Is Depressed

You can get all A's and still flunk life.

Walker Percy, *The Second Coming*

Jack did not know he was depressed. All he knew was that he was irritable most of the time and he was generally "pissed off" at life. He tried to deal with his anger by working longer hours and escaping into TV when he was home. Sometimes he drank too much. His wife attempted to talk to him about his behavior and his frequent rudeness, but he hated those "in-depth conversations." Growing up, he had never learned to talk about his feelings. His dad taught him that men were silent and strong; his mother was uncomfortable talking to him when he struggled in school or with friends. So he married a woman who had little interest in plumbing his depths. Jack had fallen into the role of listener while they were dating, and his wife talked *at* him much of the time. It seemed to work at first, but when Jack started having trouble at the office, where he was getting passed over for promotions, it stopped working at all. Jack didn't know it, but he was lost.

Jack is rather typical of most men who are depressed. While both genders share some of the same symptoms (sadness, hopelessness, fatigue, and emptiness), men may self-medicate with alcohol, become violent or abusive, and engage in risky behavior, such as reckless driving.[1] Unlike women, who are sad and cry a lot when they are depressed, a depressed man's primary symptoms may include headaches, digestive problems, irritability, or even physical pain. Because men have been raised in America to be strong and in control, they are unlikely to share their depressive feelings with anyone. They often have no idea that their discomfort is full-blown depression. Moreover, seeking treatment may make them feel ashamed and stigmatized.[2] Because most men don't sit around talking about their emotional and psychological struggles the way women do, women are much more likely to seek help from a mental health professional than men are.

Suicide

Severe depression is more likely to be lethal for men. While women attempt suicide more often than men, men are more likely to be successful when they try to kill themselves. This is because women tend to use drugs or suffocation, while men use guns. As I have already noted, Centers for Disease Control and Prevention data from 2016 showed an increase in suicide among men in the prime of life—from age forty-five to sixty-four.[3] These are hardworking men, many of whom are husbands and fathers. When they struggle with their jobs or their families, some sink into hopelessness. In a neighborhood nearby, a man in his forties who had been going through a divorce and having problems at work shot and killed himself. Months later, also nearby, a father hanged himself on the second floor of his house while his children played on the first floor. He had been out of work for a year. This is tragic and heart-breaking. We forget just how psychologically vulnerable men can be when they lose everything that is important to them.

Men Have No Language for Depression

According to Dr. Jason Young, a clinical psychologist in Raleigh, North Carolina, men have no language for depression. Young, whose private practice consists primarily of male clients, believes men are the great internalizers, and they stuff and ignore their feelings to their own detriment. When he asks them why they have come for therapy, they often make broad, generic statements: "I just feel bad" or "I'm angry all the time." Young says they have "an agitated depression" that they don't understand, and this becomes the background noise of their lives. Young, who believes that stories flesh out our sense of humanity, says that the men he sees have no story for their interior world.

Young thinks that men are not taught to express their emotions growing up, and by adulthood, they have "accumulated all these negative feelings they have no language for." He says that women talk frequently, and some of what they talk about has emotional content. "They even talk on the way to the bathroom and in the bathroom," he says, laughing. "Men don't do this; they don't go to the bathroom together."

When Young asks his male clients about their childhoods, they usually reply that they "don't remember much." He thinks this is odd and reminiscent of abused clients who block out painful memories. For example, when he asks them to describe a major childhood event, Young's clients may say they went to the Grand

Canyon (instead of reciting a painful event or psychological trauma), completely missing or avoiding the psychological implications of Young's inquiry. "These highly educated men can sound like fourth graders when they talk about their childhoods," Young states.

Young says that "men don't know how to suffer because they have been taught they must do it alone. Their interior world is disorganized." So how does he help his clients? He tells them, "'You are depressed'—even though depression is viewed as an intolerable weakness for most men—'and this depression is forcing you into an uncomfortable inner place. But this depression will be your tutor.'" Young believes that depression, despite its discomfort and pain, will teach his clients about the emotional content of their lives.

Young uses art—usually novels and music—to help his male clients get in touch with their emotions. One of his favorite tools is the song "Unpack Your Heart" by *American Idol* winner Phillip Phillips. In this song, Phillips speaks of breaking one's silence and risking being vulnerable. He sings,

Bring your secrets, bring your scars,
Bring your glory, all you are.

For a man who has accumulated anger, sorrow, and loneliness over the years and may never have shared these emotions honestly with another person, he will resonate to this song and feel it speaks to him. He might believe for the first time that he has permission to open his heart and speak freely about his feelings, his hurts, and his confusion without believing he will be rejected.

Young says that when he uses art to give men a language for their emotions, they enter a relational space with him. He becomes "one of the guys" rather than an authority uttering wisdom, so when he says, "I'm with you," sometimes these men tear up. "We go to the top of Everest together and come back," Young says. As Young works with his depressed clients, they begin to acquire a whole new way of speaking to express the wide range of their emotions, not just their anger. He says that "they begin to get a new voice and can speak in a new way." Young feels they come to see their emotions as friends who will help them experience more of life and live in the present. He often quotes from Walker Percy's *The Second Coming* because he says it teaches clients about living in the moment rather than living in the past or the future. Here's his favorite quote from Percy's novel:

> How did it happen that now he could see everything so clearly? Something had given him leave to live in the present. Not once in his entire life had he come to rest in the quiet center of himself but had forever cast himself from some dark past he could not remember to a future that did not exist. *Not once had he been present in his life.* So his life had passed like a dream. Is it possible for people to miss their lives the way one can miss a plane?[4]

Young wants his depressed clients to experience the present and avoid missing out on their lives. He is, however, well aware that he is not the only one helping his clients emerge from the darkness: "God's spirit is at work in their lives. And His creativity is too complicated for there to be only one way to help clients deal with depression."

As for his part in the healing process, Young likes to quote his father-in-law, an engineer, who says, "All physical problems have a solution." But, Young explains, "the problem with emotions is that they aren't governed by the same laws. Therefore, we are on a journey without a clear road map. We have to find the language that automatically communicates what a man is feeling." He continues, "I'm fascinated by that process. So with my clients, we start to tinker until we find a solution."

Finally, Young believes that depressed people often get better because their life circumstances change: "Therapy adds to this in that they begin to have a new voice and can speak in a new way, and they begin to see that even their negative emotions are friends." In the process, Young says, "they discover a new way to experience more of life."

Judy's Story

To show what it's like to have a depressed husband, I'll share Judy's story. Because substance abuse is often associated with clinical depression, this interview—honest and raw—should provide some help in dealing with the tangled problems of alcohol and depression.

Judy has been married to Roy for thirty years, and for much of that time, he has been depressed and intermittently dependent on alcohol. He has only been completely sober for the last three years. Both Judy and Roy are smart and educated and have worked as doctors, and though she had an early and stellar career in medicine, Judy became a stay-at-home mother when the first of her three sons was born.

Judy begins our interview by saying that she is "a positive, solution-oriented, can-do person." However, it wasn't easy for her to be an empathic, compassionate partner for Roy, who, at his worst, would go to the office and then "come home, throw himself on the couch, eat dinner with the family, and disappear." She feels it would have been better for their sons to have a father who was involved in their lives. "My children suffered from a great lack of presence," Judy says. "I needed Roy's participation in the lives of our active sons; I needed him to sometimes take them to sports practice." She continues, "It was really, really hard to endure—to do it in a way so that I would not sour the children's opinion of their dad. It was like threading a difficult needle." She found it increasingly hard to keep it all together during Roy's bouts of depression and his "falling off the wagon intermittently." Judy admits that she wanted to bail several times and that it was only because of God's grace that she stayed in the marriage and was able to continue to love Roy.

How did she experience Roy's clinical depression? "Roy had a terrible temper, and at times, he was unkind to our son James, the oldest. Once, James lost it and told Roy how much he hated him. It was horrible, horrible." Judy admits that she has lots of bad memories that she consciously chooses not to rehearse. She says this period lasted for years, and though Roy took an antidepressant and saw a psychiatrist from time to time, he refused to go to talk therapy: "He visited several psychologists once or twice but said, 'That person didn't help me. I am never going back.'"

How did Judy, an accomplished, can-do person, manage to mother her sons and hope that someday her marriage would get better? Mainly, she changed the way she viewed her life. While she described herself as "tenaciously optimistic" prior to becoming a Christian, her troubled marriage demanded a new and deeper perspective.

Judy finally decided that she couldn't change Roy, but she was going to have "a great life anyway." She immersed herself in organizations, her boys' activities, and friendships with other women. Soon her life was "full of good things and good people." She knew this was her coping mechanism, her way of handling her husband's depressive thinking and alcoholism.

Mostly, she concentrated on her faith. Judy is a Catholic and goes to mass six days a week. She says, "I would go feeling anxious, weepy, despairing; I would come out of mass, having taken communion, and I would be at peace." She adds, "It was 100 percent reliable." She believed God would provide all she didn't have and that He would guide her and get her through the day. A mentor of hers, a wise priest, reminded her that when she married Roy, she had made a vow before God and others. He told her, "Now live up to that vow." Judy knew that no matter how she felt at times, she could not break her vow to God to love her husband until death. Judy said that when she couldn't do it anymore, God took over, encouraging her and keeping hope alive.

Three years ago, the family had an intervention for Roy, and on that occasion, Judy feels God broke Roy's obsession with alcohol: "This time it was real and deep. The boys were present at the intervention, and they told their father what his alcoholism and depression felt like to them. Basically, they said they had wanted to help him, to be compassionate, to be able to write an honest Father's Day card—but now they were done. Roy got the message. He changed. He has been sober ever since."

After the intervention, Judy and Roy, who had been married for twenty-seven years, went to an Imago Weekend Workshop for couples, and that made a significant difference in their marriage. Roy wept when he started talking about his mother during an exercise at the workshop. "When he wept, something inside me softened," Judy says. Roy simply couldn't bring himself to talk about his mother because his wounds were too deep: "Roy couldn't trust. I always knew he had a mother problem, but he wouldn't talk about her. I felt he unloaded his anger and confusion about her onto me. I would say, 'Hey, we're on the same team.' But it made no difference." Judy continues, "I have always felt we had three people in this marriage."

What about Roy's dad? "Roy's mom was superstrong, but his dad was afraid of her. He stayed clear of her. Roy had lots of resentment toward his dad because he refused to tell Roy's mother to knock it off," Judy says. She feels that Roy's attachment relationship with his mother fueled his depression and cynicism: "His is the glass half empty. Consequently, he has had difficulty trusting his family and God."

The Imago Weekend Workshop allowed Judy to process her feelings toward Roy and helped her show compassion and empathy toward him, emotions Roy desperately needed to experience. It also gave both of them a way of communicating deeply with each other. In an exercise at the end of the weekend, Roy told Judy all the reasons he loved her. He said that he loved her for "things that were lovable and true"—things she didn't even know he was aware of. Until that time, Judy did not feel valued by Roy based on the way he treated her. "I came home from the weekend feeling he really loved me," she says. At the Imago Weekend Workshop, she learned from the therapists and participants that she was exactly the right person for Roy and he was just as right for her. That truth has made a profound difference in their marriage. Now Roy trusts her; he knows he put her through the mill and has told her she had every right to walk out, but she didn't. He believes that if he stays sober, she's "sticking around."

Last year, Judy and Roy had a little grandson, their first, and now Roy realizes he can't go around being a "jerk." He was touched when his oldest son, who once said he hated Roy, named his first child after his father. Whenever he holds his adorable grandson, Roy feels it's imperative that he live up to his son's and his daughter-in-law's trust.

Because of the healing and redemption that has occurred in the past three years, Judy is optimistic about her marriage and her future with Roy. Their sons are grown and gone; now it is just the two of them. They sold their large, award-winning family home in Chicago and are building a much smaller one. "This is not just about downsizing," she says. "It's also about creating a beautiful new start in our lives."

So What Does This Have to Do with You?

I have shared Judy's story because substance abuse is all too often part of the fabric of male depression, and in my office, I have seen the horrific pain this powerful combination causes wives and children. Their anger, sorrow, and helplessness in trying to get the alcoholic to change are palpable. Thankfully, Judy was willing to share her story and to tell us just how difficult it was to stay in the marriage and to hope that life would ever get better. Moreover, she has been absolutely clear about one thing: it was her intimate relationship with Christ, strengthened by her daily taking of communion, that allowed her to love Roy through the dark times, help raise their stalwart sons, and create a fulfilling life for herself in the process.

Perhaps you, dear reader, can draw strength from her example.

CHAPTER FOUR

When a Woman Is Depressed

A woman is like a tea bag. You can't tell how strong
she is until you put her in hot water.

Eleanor Roosevelt

Maybe you have to know the darkness before you can appreciate the light.
Madeleine L'Engle, *A Ring of Endless Light*

When I was thirty-seven years old and in the third year of my second marriage, I became seriously depressed. It was as if the unaddressed hurts from earlier in my life had decided it was finally time to roll in to haunt me. I had the classic symptoms of women who are moderately to severely depressed: I felt sad and empty, anxious, tired all the time, unable to sleep, and worthless. My husband, Don, and I had just moved to New Jersey, leaving friends and work behind in Asheville, North Carolina. My girls were enrolled in elementary school and junior high. When the three of them went off to their various lives in the morning—Don to his job and the girls to school—I found myself, an educated woman, living in a small town without a job or any work I wanted to do.

I had already published my first book, *Beyond Divorce*, and probably should have attempted to write another book during my solitary days. But at an unconscious level, it seemed that my mind understood that since I had found a safe harbor in my second marriage, it was time to deal with the past—all the losses and ruptured attachments. During my solitary days, I remembered. I remembered the losses of childhood, the difficulties of leaving the stability of my grandparents' farm for life with my emotionally unstable mother, the betrayal by my first husband when I had two babies to care for. My days were full of dark memories and unaddressed pain.

During that season of darkness, Don came to my rescue. He showed me great empathy, listening as I chronicled all the hurts. He soothed my pain; he offered hope. Although he had never been clinically depressed himself, he stretched to understand and show compassion. Having grown up in a stable and loving two-parent home, Don has always had amazing resilience in dealing with the exigencies of life. One day, when I felt especially low, my ambitious husband took off work and we hiked a nearby part of the Appalachian Trail while the girls were in school. He packed a picnic lunch, and we made love in the afternoon. I will never forget that day.

In time, the darkness lifted and I found my way. But it was not until I was diagnosed with breast cancer at age fifty-seven that I finally sought help from a psychologist and dealt with my painful, conflictual relationship with Mother. Working through that and severing the ball and chain I had dragged through life is, I am convinced, part of the reason I am alive today.

Women and Depression

Women are familiar with depression. Studies suggest that females are twice as likely as men to become depressed and that one in four women will experience an episode of depression once in her lifetime.[1] When women are depressed, they are irritable and quick to anger and often feel worthless. They are hard to live with. A husband, when asked how he felt living with a depressed wife, said he could handle his wife's feelings of helplessness (after all, he saw himself as a knight on a white horse), but he could not manage her anger: "Over time, her anger wears me down, and I am not as patient as I would naturally be." He felt that all he could do was leave his wife's presence and wait for the anger to pass.

If you, dear reader, have a mother who suffers from depression, or an adolescent or adult daughter who is depressed, you know that some days you have to dodge the bullets. Said one mother, "I can feel pretty good, but minutes after my depressed fourteen-year-old daughter walks in the door, my own mood plummets." On the other hand, how many adolescent daughters, who are themselves struggling with low self-esteem, find it hard to deal with their depressed mothers in those hours after the school day ends? The truth is that it is hard to be around *any* woman who is struggling with depression.

Not only do women experience the usual causes of depression (stress, the loss of a loved one, career setbacks, an unhappy marriage), but women's fluctuating hormones add to the mix. Starting in puberty, women are assailed by their hormones as they begin to menstruate until they have gone through menopause. Women are, to some extent, victims of hormonal challenges. This is not to say we cannot attempt to manage our moods, especially around menstruation, but we are cognizant of hormonal challenges, and many women are grateful to get to the other side of menopause.

If you have a depressed woman in your life, read on. If you love a woman or are married to one, you may learn more than you ever knew about gender differences, the way someone you love is affected by her hormones, and the easy intimacy that women have in talking about their biological selves, especially with other women. Even if you had a close relationship with the first woman you ever loved, your mother, you probably feel like a twenty-year-old friend of mine who, though well loved by the women in his life, said, "Women will always be a mystery to me."

Women and Hormones

Often women are a mystery to themselves. What woman does not remember the middle school years, when she left childhood behind and sallied into the realm of zits, dicey friendships, braces, and—the bane of her existence—self-consciousness and its little sister, low self-esteem? Try to tell a middle school girl that there is no unseen audience—that the girls she knows are focused on *their* weight, *their* zits, and *their* popularity, not on hers—and she will look at you incredulously. She believes that everyone knows exactly how she feels about herself and that they will judge her because she is not beautiful and popular. It's in middle school that girls first learn that someone is smarter, a better athlete, or more popular than they are. In this painful period of life, some get voted off the lunch table or out of the group, or a girl sees on Instagram that a friend had a birthday party and did not invite her. Women learn early on what it feels like to be rejected by peers, and, boy, does it hurt. Who does not remember the angst of the middle school years?

All our lives—until we are beyond menopause—we are affected more than we know by our hormones. Take pregnancy. While some women are thrilled to carry new life, others may experience mild or even moderate depression and need to consult their primary providers about possible treatment. Some pregnant women can profit from psychotherapy to help unravel the causes of depression.

While pregnancy causes the hormones to dance, affecting a woman's brain chemistry as well as the shape of her body, it is important for the woman in your life to examine her feelings and attitudes toward her pregnancy. Is this a baby she welcomes? Is this the right time to start a family or enlarge an existing one? If you are her husband, do you have a good marriage, and are you excited about the pregnancy? Does she worry about balancing mother-hood with a demanding career?

But pregnancy might do more than cause anxiety about the future; it can also dredge up the past. This is a question I always ask women who come to me mildly depressed and pregnant: *How's your relationship with your mother?* Why do I ask this question? *Because pregnancy and childbirth invariably take a woman "home" psychologically.* She revisits her childhood and her earliest attach-ments, even if only unconsciously. If she was raised by nurturing parents, particularly her mother, then she will most likely wel-come her baby and anticipate the birth. If, on the other hand, she lost her mother—whether her mother died, abandoned her, or is otherwise estranged from her—then the pregnancy becomes prob-lematic. This woman is likely to feel troubled and conflicted. After all, as an expectant mother, she identifies more closely with her own mother than she has before. While this can have a positive effect on some mother-daughter relationships, it can also evoke pain and anxiety in a woman who does not have a warm and affectionate relationship with her mother. If this is the case, it can be healing to find an older, nurturing female therapist to work with and begin to examine the painful mother-daughter bond. You might encourage your wife to seek help if her pregnancy creates depressive thoughts and feelings. You can also assure her that you will be with her both physically and emotionally throughout the experience and that the two of you will get through this time together. The husband's role is to encircle his wife and the unborn child with loving care and protection. This is a good time to bring your wife a cup of tea or coffee as a nurturing act. While this may sound absurdly simple, this small act of kindness can let your wife know that you want to be empathic and help her through this time.

I have worked with many younger women over the years who have had painful relationships with their mothers and have found that pregnancy is a good time (a "pregnant" time) to work on the mother-daughter bond. As these clients process their pain, learn to set healthy boundaries, address Mom's criticism, forgive, and come to accept what their flawed mothers have to give, whether a little or a lot, something beautiful happens. Positive emotions begin to surface. These women become realistic about what they can expect from their mothers while at the same time acknowledging their own yearning for mothering. I often suggest they find an experienced mother to teach them how to care for their baby and at the same time provide some nurturing for them. Basically, whenever a woman has a baby, she will need someone to nurture her.

Postpartum Depression

Some women will go on to have postpartum depression during the days, weeks, and even months after the birth of a child. While most new mothers will have days when they are moody or tired and anxious, these symptoms usually resolve within days or a few weeks. Some women, however, become severely depressed within four weeks postpartum. They may have crying spells, sleepless nights, depressed moods, fatigue, high anxiety, and an inability to concentrate. Risk factors for postpartum depression include depression during pregnancy, stress associated with caring for a baby, a lack of social support, general life stress, prenatal anxiety, marital unhappiness, and a history of prior depression.[2]

Several celebrities have admitted that they experienced postpartum depression. Gwyneth Paltrow, Courtney Cox, and Brooke Shields have all said that they grappled with this maternal illness. In fact, Brooke Shields's book *Down Came the Rain: My Journey through Postpartum Depression* chronicles this painful experience. She also wrote an op-ed for the *New York Times* on the subject in response to Tom Cruise's diatribe against antidepressants on the *Today* show. While he advocated vitamins and exercise for postpartum depression, Shields challenged his perspective by recounting her own story.

Shields says she had expected to be overjoyed by her pregnancy. After all, she had tried to get pregnant for two years and had even made several attempts with in vitro fertilization. Instead, when her daughter Rowan Francis Henchy was born in 2003, she felt overwhelmed: "This baby was a stranger to me. I didn't know what to do with her. I didn't feel at all joyful. I attributed feelings of doom to simple fatigue and figured that they would eventually go away. But they didn't; in fact, they got worse."[3] She admits that she wanted her baby to "disappear" and she herself wanted to vanish. Shields had suicidal thoughts, and once, when she stopped taking Paxil, she had a relapse and wanted to drive her car into a wall with her baby in the back seat. Shields believes that antidepressants and talk therapy saved her and her family.[4]

Some women suffer from an extreme and rare kind of postpartum depression called "postpartum depression with psychosis." Cindy Wachenheim, a Manhattan lawyer with the state supreme court, finally became a mother when she had a baby boy in her forties, and she wanted to be the "perfect" mother. When her baby was four months old, he had a minor fall while pushing himself up on a play mat. Cindy became obsessive, believing that this incident caused him to have severe neurological problems. She blamed herself for placing the play mat on the hardwood floor. Two pediatric neurologists assured her that the baby was normal, but she remained delusional, convinced that she had harmed her baby and he would never be normal. Those who loved her—her husband and her siblings—urged her to seek therapy. She saw a psychiatrist, was put on Zoloft, and found out that she was suffering from postpartum depression with psychosis, a rare illness that affects one to two mothers out of one thousand. A small percentage of these women end up hurting their children or killing themselves.[5]

Despite treatment, Cindy remained convinced she had hurt her son, that he would never walk as a result, and that he had suffered a concussion. Although Cindy's sister and husband kept close watch on her, one day, Cindy strapped her ten-month-old son to her body and jumped from an eight-story window. Heartbreakingly, she died. However, her body cushioned her baby's fall and saved his life. Within a few weeks, he took his first steps.[6]

Cindy's story illustrates the fact that a mother can develop postpartum depression with psychosis months after the birth of her baby and that, sadly, sometimes concerned loved ones and even a psychiatrist cannot keep her alive. If you believe someone you love has postpartum depression or postpartum depression with psychosis, encourage her to seek treatment immediately and to surround herself with other new moms to help normalize some of her feelings. Then, in addition to seeing a psychiatrist for an antidepressant or antianxiety medication, she should find an older, nurturing therapist who has raised her own children and who can help her with this significant life transition. Too much time alone is counterproductive; it just gives the depressed new mom more time to obsess about her worries and fears.

Menopause

Another time when women experience hormonal shifts occurs in the years leading up to menopause, when hormones are decreasing and are, as one woman said, "bouncing off the walls." Since most women cease menstruation around age fifty, the years leading up to menopause can be rocky. Sometimes clients come in complaining of headaches, insomnia, mild depression, hot flashes, and lots of anxiety. "I feel like the sky is falling on Chicken Little," said one client sheepishly, "and I really have nothing in my life to be this anxious about." Women often fail to connect the dots and understand that their decreasing estrogen levels are causing some of their symptoms.

Now is the time to have a gynecologist check hormonal levels and learn about the symptoms of menopause.

While hot flashes, increased headaches, and irregular periods alert a woman to the approach of menopause, some husbands feel they are married to a depressed and anxious alien who bears little resemblance to their former wife. One baffled husband was convinced that either his wife had a split personality or she had developed a new personality when she approached fifty. He created a T-shirt for her that said on the front, "She wouldn't take estrogen," and on the back, "So I did."—all in good fun. If the two of you can find any humor in the situation, believe me, it helps to laugh.

Once a client came to see me and said that she was nearing menopause. She was forty-nine and had begun to have severe hot flashes—when she led meetings or gave speeches, sweat trickled down her legs. That morning, she had gone to the high school where she coached basketball, and a fellow teacher, also menopausal, said to her in the teacher's lounge, "You drive, I'll shoot." We had a good laugh and then spoke of deeper things. I assure women that once they pass the great divide and stop menstruating, they will feel mellower and have greater self-confidence.

For many, the hormonal headaches will cease, and although hot flashes may continue, most women find a way to deal with them. It's a bit like descending the mountain that a woman spends part of her forties rigorously climbing.

Encourage the Woman in Your Life

These are the years for excellent plant-based nutrition, exercise, girlfriends, sufficient sleep, and stress reduction. (Stress makes everything worse during this period of life.) It is also the time to work on a marriage that may have been neglected during the intense years of child-rearing. Since an unhappy union has been linked to cancer, heart disease, and depression in women, this is the time for couples therapy if the woman you love feels the marriage has tanked. Not only is marital misery acutely stressful, but it's also debilitating. Counseling—both marital and individual—can prove invaluable as a woman goes over her hormonal Niagara Falls in a barrel.

A positive way to view all the hormonal shifts women experience is to understand that women are often reinventing themselves as they move through the various stages of female development. In fact, women tend to reinvent themselves more often than men. As a female grows from child to young girl to woman, she may become a worker, lover, adventurer, and mother, and then in her fifties, when she approaches menopause, she can begin to nurture the next generation and contribute to culture with greater freedom of mind.

When a woman enters her sixties, she enters a rich period of life—a stage of grace where no one expects great things from her and people are surprised that she continues to use her substantial gifts to enrich society. A friend told me recently that after I told her this, she felt empowered and liberated. Nancy has used her own substantial gifts in shaping people's world views and the culture in her late sixties and early seventies. She has a cause—save America—and she is passionate about it.

And should she reach her seventies, a woman will don the wise-woman role and help those behind her, the younger ones, who come seeking her wisdom. This is the time for her to start a Women of Wisdom (WOW) group of peers to talk about the challenges (and there are many) of her abundant life. If a woman can stay productive and keep herself out of the depression pit, these can be fulfilling years to share the knowledge she has gleaned throughout her life.

Women live fascinating lives. Granted, a woman needs to learn to manage her moods—her anxiety and negative thinking (which tend to dissipate with age). Usually, women grow stronger emotionally as they age. If a woman has addressed the wounds of the past and if she keeps short accounts in the present, if she has learned to forgive and ask for forgiveness, then the latter part of life can be exceedingly rich. Women in their seventies and eighties tell me repeatedly that they want to be productive until they "drop."

A woman can, with God's help, create a life that sings.

CHAPTER FIVE

When Your Adolescent Is Depressed

*Studies have found that adolescent depression is not the transitory,
benign condition is has been presumed to be. Depressive symptoms
have been linked to adolescent suicidal behavior, a phenomenon
that has increased dramatically during the past two decades.*

Joan F. Robertson and Ronald L Simons,
Journal of Marriage and Family

Few things are more frightening to a parent than having a depressed teenager.

A sensitive parent lives each day conscious of the culture his child swims in with its smartphones, Xboxes, social media, gender confusion, and steady rollout of sex and violence on television and in movies. Add to the mix heavy academic pressure that becomes intense in eleventh and twelfth grades, with its accompanying sleep deprivation, and it's easy to have an unhappy kid. So when a mother sees her fifteen-year-old daughter retreat to her bedroom in a bad mood or hears her talk about feeling friendless every time she sees photos posted online from a party she wasn't invited to, that mother worries. Is Sarah just experiencing typical adolescent mood swings, especially around her period, or is she depressed? And when Scott goes silent, loses weight, spends too much time alone, and almost always looks unhappy, his mother may ask herself if his life is just too stressful or if he is depressed.

Even therapists sometimes have difficulty figuring out if a teenager is depressed or just swamped with all the developmental changes that occur in adolescence. After all, these are the years in early adolescence that hormones kick in and the self-consciousness of middle school breeds angst. In addition, adolescents are bombarded by so much more in the culture today than forty or fifty years ago. *Then* kids experienced self-doubt, the desire to be popular, the need to make good grades and go to college—but without technology, they did not sleep with their smartphones, constantly staring at their screens, nor did they experience cyberbullying. Adolescents today must cope with radical changes in American culture, and it sometimes takes a significant toll. In addition, they have "never known a time when terrorism and school shootings weren't the norm."[1]

In fact, Susanna Schrobsdorff, writing in *Time* magazine, says that "adolescents today have a reputation for being more fragile, less resilient and more overwhelmed than their parents were when they were growing up."[2] Schrobsdorff continues, "In 2015, about 3 million teens ages 12 to 17 had had at least one major depressive episode in the past year, according to the Department of Health and Human Services. More than 2 million report experiencing depression that impairs their daily function. About 30% of girls and 20% of boys—totaling 6.3 million teens—have had an anxiety disorder, according to data from the National Institutes of Mental Health."[3]

One of the transformative factors in a teenager's life today is social media. Janis Whitlock, director of the Cornell Research Program on Self-Injury and Recovery, believes the epidemic of mood disorders for teens is driven less by what's happening in the culture than by technology and social media. She says, "It's that they're in a cauldron of stimulus they can't get away from, or don't want to get away from, or don't know how to get away from." Faith Ann, a twenty-year-old who began cutting herself when she was in high school, hiding sadness she couldn't articulate to her parents, says, "We're the first generation that cannot escape our problems at all."[4]

It may be hard for you as a parent to understand the ramifications of technology in your children's lives. Not only can your children not escape technology, but it exposes them to everything sexual and predatory while promising them friendship and intimacy it cannot deliver. As Sherry Turkle, an MIT researcher and author of the book *Alone Together: Why We Expect More from Technology and Less from Each Other*, says, "Technology is seductive when what it offers meets our human vulnerabilities. As it turns out, we are very vulnerable indeed. We are lonely but fearful of intimacy. Digital connections and the sociable robot may offer the illusion of companionship without the demands of friendship. Our networked life allows us to hide from each other, even as we are tethered to each other. We'd rather text than talk."[5]

This loss of intimacy in human relationships in American culture has been profound. The loss can be seen in marriages, in parent-child relationships, and often in friendships. I notice it in my work with clients who contact me for therapy and speak of "communication problems." This is client-speak for the absence of intimacy. An even more troubling sign is the loss of eye contact. Some clients refuse to look at me when they first come for therapy; their eyes wander around the room as they speak. Yet eye contact is established in infancy and is a profound indicator of the level of trust and emotional security that a baby has in his emotional bond with his mother and father. I notice that, over time, these clients slowly begin to look at me as they begin to trust me, and I make the absence of eye contact a therapy issue. How is your teen's eye contact? Does he look at you when he speaks? Do you look at her?

Technology makes eye contact or face-to-face encounters even harder, often leaving kids feeling lonely and empty inside. This is especially true since teens often do not understand that the "friendship" they experience on Facebook is illusory. Sometimes, even as they stare at their screens, searching avidly and frequently for messages from friends, they may feel sad and empty inside. This sadness—this inability to have an intimate, nourishing, and *real* encounter with another person—can lead to anxiety and depression.

Warning Signs

So how can you tell if your teenager is depressed? According to the Mayo Clinic, a sensitive and observant parent should look for the following warning signs when a teen appears lost and unhappy. Is your child

- talking or writing about suicide?
- withdrawing from friends and family?
- experiencing mood swings?
- using alcohol or drugs?

- feeling hopeless?
- changing eating and sleeping patterns?
- giving away belongings?
- acting severely anxious and agitated?[6]

If your teen displays some or all of these warning signs, it's important to take these signs seriously and not discount them as moodiness or assume tomorrow will be a better day. Now is the time to find an empathic therapist who is trained in working with adolescents. *Pronto.*

Suicide Rates and Our Children

Why this alarm? Suicide rates have risen for teens in America. According to the Centers for Disease Control and Prevention (CDC), suicide rates have risen 200 percent since 1999 for girls ages ten to fourteen. Suicide rates for males were also higher in 2014 than in 1999 for all age groups younger than seventy-five. Females took their lives predominately through poisoning, and males used guns.[7]

Because adolescents are often impulsive and immature, the danger of suicide may be real depending on the severity of the depression. The Centers for Disease Control and Prevention Youth Risk Behavior Surveillance survey released in June of 2016 reported that nationally, some 17.7 percent of American students seriously considered attempting suicide in the previous twelve months. More females (23.4 percent) than males (12.2 percent) had seriously thought about killing themselves. The group with the highest percentage was ninth-grade girls (26.5 percent).[8] Imagine that—a fourth of the ninth-grade girls surveyed had wanted to die. While experts suggest that the reasons for this dramatic upsurge in suicide for ten- to fourteen-year-old girls are the stagnant economy, earlier puberty, and cyberbullying, among others, I would like to suggest that something else is going on.

It's Hard to Be a Girl Today

If you are the mother of a daughter, you know that it's difficult to be female today. Last winter, I was coming out of Nordstrom and saw a beautiful girl with long black hair, stylish clothes, and the latest boots sitting on a bench. We struck up a conversation about just how hard it is to find clothes we like that suit our actual bodies, and soon we drifted into why it's hard to be female in this culture. She said softly, "It's hard to be a girl today. You have to wear the right clothes; your hair needs to look a certain way. You have to get into the right college, be on social media, and please your parents. And when you go to college, there's the pressure to hook up. A girl does it, and sometimes she drinks to be able to do it because she thinks she will lose her boyfriend if she doesn't have sex with him. But she loses him anyway. And then she cries."

As I walked to my car, I was struck by this young woman's poignant commentary. I could sense her vulnerability, sadness, and wistfulness. Perhaps she was one of those pretty girls who engaged in hooking up in high school or college and suffered the fallout in terms of shame and loss of self-esteem. As I drove off, I agreed with her. It *is* hard to be a girl today. From middle school through college, girls in America have so many pressures on them to be smart, hang with the popular kids, and have sex. Moreover, they must please their parents by getting into the right college or university.

It's overwhelming. It can be devastating.

Apparently, ninth-grade girls feel this keenly.

Silicon Valley Suicides

Sometimes our kids just can't cope with all the social and academic pressure they feel as they build resumes for college admission. Hanna Rosin wrote an article for the *Atlantic Monthly* entitled "The Silicon Valley Suicides" about the suicides at Henry M. Gunn High School, a school of 1,900 students in California: "It was November 4, 2014, a few days after homecoming and maybe a month before college applications would start making everyone crazy. The teacher read a statement containing the words *took his own life last night*, and then a name, Cameron Lee. Alyssa's first thought: *Is there another Cameron Lee at our school?*, because the one she knew was popular and athletic and seemingly unbothered by schoolwork, an avid practitioner of the annoying prank of turning people's backpacks inside out."[9] Lee had jumped in front of the speeding Caltrain, a commuter train that comes into Silicon Valley several times during a twenty-four-hour period. He was not the first student to end his life by leaping in front of the speeding train. Over a period of nine months starting in the spring of 2009, three Gunn students had killed themselves this way, as had one incoming freshman and one recent graduate. Another recent graduate had hanged himself. Gunn and another high school, Palo Alto High, reported a suicide rate between four and five times the national average over a ten-year period.[10] This area of the world has had its "suicide clusters," defined by Rosin as "multiple deaths in close succession and proximity."

A Word to Parents

The same day that Lee jumped in front of a train, Martha Cabot, also a student at Gunn, posted a YouTube video in which she urged parents to "calm down" and not push their children so much.[11] She noted that while four AP classes, two junior year and two senior year, should be enough for a college-bound student, seven was the social norm at the award-winning high school. Cabot lamented the stress and pressure that she and her classmates experienced daily. She said the stress of getting high grades, having a full social life, and participating in sports and clubs is "ridiculous." She also said that most seniors at Gunn have fifteen backup schools when they apply for college.

What kind of community do Gunn students come from? Looking at the student body, 74 percent have at least one parent with a graduate degree. These are high-achieving parents. And every year, a number of Gunn students go to Stanford and University of California schools—in particular, Berkeley. These kids are among the best and brightest in the nation. Rosin asks, "Had parents really given their kids the idea that they had to perform? That their love had to be earned with A's and Advanced Placement tests and trophies? They hadn't meant to." Yet, as Rosin writes, academic pressure can cause anxiety and depression, which have been linked to suicide.[12]

Assistant Professor Suniya Luthar from Yale's psychiatry group later came to Palo Alto to speak on affluent kids as an at-risk group. She has studied inner-city kids as well as the children of affluent parents. She found that the wealthier students smoked, drank, and used hard drugs at a significantly higher rate than students in inner-city schools did. While they were no more likely to kill themselves than poorer kids, the children of the affluent reported clinically significant anxiety and depression two to three times higher than the national average. This researcher also found that children of the affluent felt isolated from their busy parents, who were often absent from the home during afternoons and evenings. She discovered that children in affluent communities felt "their parents to be no more available to them, either emotionally or physically, than the kids in severe poverty did."[13]

Luthar "constructed a profile of elite American adolescents whose self-worth is tied to their achievements and who see themselves as catastrophically flawed if they don't meet the highest standards of success." And though they were not emotionally close to their often absent parents, the children of the affluent had nevertheless internalized their parents' priorities to their own detriment.[14]

When academic pressure exists without emotional closeness, it can be a potentially lethal mix.

If Your Child Is Depressed

If you think your teenager is depressed, have him or her evaluated by a psychiatrist who can put your child on an antidepressant. Since I, as a psychologist, cannot prescribe medication, I spoke with North Carolina psychiatrist Dr. Collette Ah-Tye, board certified in both adult and adolescent psychiatry, about treating adolescent depression. She says she is biased in favor of medication when she determines an adolescent is depressed. "My patients are possibly suicidal when they get to me," she says. "They have often been depressed for a year or two, so I feel blessed to have SSRIs to prescribe."

Ah-Tye says she often starts with Prozac and goes "low and slow." She says, "The worst thing is to go too high and have the patient have a bad experience. I want the patient to have a positive experience and avoid side effects." She adds that if there will be adverse reactions, she will usually see them within a month. She doesn't want a big change in the teenager's mood: "A little bit better each month is perfect."

Ah-Tye encourages parents to get support while their teenager is in therapy, particularly if they are worried about suicide risk. When asked about ways parents can help, she says that once they get professional help for their child, they should consider getting help for themselves. She believes parents need to learn to manage conflict with their child. She also wants to know if Mom and Dad have conflicts that are getting played out through their offspring. She mentions that it is harmful to the child if divorced parents try to work out their conflicts through their child. Ah-Tye believes in parental supervision and says kids don't need too much down time. "When my patients can find healthy, nondestructive ways to experience life, I am thrilled," she says.

Just because He Exists

At this point, I need to say that it's important that you love your child just because he exists, not because of anything he achieves. *Any time you marry love and acceptance with performance, you are headed for trouble.* Big trouble. I have counseled some bright high achievers from top universities who ended up in my office complaining of depression; they felt they had never been good enough or accomplished enough, even though their accomplishments would put them in the top 1 percent in the nation.

Remember how you felt when you first held your baby in your arms? At that time, she had achieved nothing. That baby was just your beloved child. You loved her just because she was yours and she existed. Try now to remember how you felt, and tell your daughter you love her just because she exists and belongs to you. A friend of mine has a daughter—Sim, a freshman at UCLA—whom she adopted from Vietnam. When asked what her name means, this confident young woman replies, "My grandmother says it means *She Is Marvelous.*" In fact, when Sim wrote her personal statement for her college applications, she explained the meaning of her name and said that when her mother, Ellen, came to Vietnam to adopt her, the locals who saw this Caucasian woman carrying a Vietnamese baby down the streets of Hanoi came up and said, "Lucky baby." Sim wrote that she has been lucky indeed to have her mom as her mentor; moreover, she embraces her grandmother's explanation of the meaning of her name.

Your child is also marvelous, just as he sits, walks, and stands.

Parents who love their kids for who they are and not for their accomplishments or admission to elite colleges have emotionally secure and resilient kids. These are the kids who can experience setbacks, get a low grade, feel disappointed because they did not get into the college of their choice, sleep on it, and bounce back in the morning. You and your teenager need to remember that there is life after college, and part of the reason to go to college is to have fun and leave the nest.

And do be careful about your daily absence from her life. Your child or teenager needs you for some part of her day. And if you cannot be with her when she walks through the door, then call her and talk long enough that she feels heard. At bedtime, if you have been absent in the afternoon, pull up a chair beside her bed and ask her about her day. Be prepared to stay awhile and listen. Check in on her life and her emotional state. Make it safe for your son or daughter to tell you about her worries, her troubles, her wild and wooly thoughts. Often when kids cut themselves, they live in families where they cannot discuss negative feelings, so the cutting temporarily relieves psychological pain. I suggest that parents spend ten to fifteen minutes each day alone with their child just listening to any hurts, troubles, or worries. As you help your child process any pain, this act can prevent a world of trouble.

If you believe you are putting too much pressure on your child to achieve, then ask yourself the following questions: Do I feel happy about *my* accomplishments in life? What is driving me? Is my self-worth too tightly tied to my child's accomplishments? Then reflect on your past: Did you have parents who loved you just because you existed, or were you pushed mercilessly? Perhaps you feel you sacrificed your dreams to rear your child and this may be payback time. Of course, you may not be conscious of these undercurrents in your emotional life as you apply academic and social pressure to your son or daughter. Now is a good time to become more self-aware and understand where all this pressure you and your child feel comes from. It is my conviction that staying emotionally close to your teenager is the best protection you can give him. And if you have trouble doing this, find help for the two of you to strengthen your relationship.

One eighteen-year-old said she did not have sex with her boyfriend in high school because whenever she was tempted, she could envision her mother's face, and she did not want to hurt the mother she loved who had poured her life into her daughter. It's the close emotional bond we have with our children that makes them want to live lives we, their parents, can respect.

Final Thoughts

Now for some practical counsel.

First, carefully monitor your child's screen time. When Kristen Blair and I wrote *From Santa to Sexting: Helping Your Child Safely Navigate Middle School and Shape the Choices That Last a Lifetime*, we found that many parents were reluctant to set limits on their child's use of technology. We were surprised and somewhat dismayed. In our book, we suggested that kids should come to the dinner table without their smartphones and that they should relinquish them at study time and at bedtime. No one needs to sleep with a smartphone that awakens him with each incoming text message. Experts who work with kids say that smartphones keep kids "hyperconnected" and "overexposed," and this can create great anxiety.

Second, make sure you obey any rules you establish for your kids. Megan Moreno, head of social media and adolescent health research at Seattle Children's Hospital, says that often parents "mimic" their kids' behavior. "They're zoning out. ... They're answering calls during dinner rather than saying, 'O.K., we have this technology. Here are the rules about when we use it.'"[15] In your heart, you know you cannot ask for anything from your kids that you are unwilling to do yourself.

Third, give your girls strategies for solving their social problems. A 2017 study of 123 middle schoolers, as well as parents and teachers, found that when parents gave their daughters strategies for finding friends—such as joining a school club with kids who had similar interests—they developed stronger friendships.[16]

Finally, make sure she gets most of the sleep she needs. Cameron Lee never seemed to sleep. His classmates said they could call him in the middle of the night and he would be awake. He blamed his sleeplessness on having to do homework, though he was also on Twitter and Snapchat late at night. We will never know how sleep deprivation played into his decision to leap in front of a train[17] or how it influences any feelings of hopelessness that kids who kill themselves inevitably have. Rest is greatly underrated in our culture, but we need those hours of repose so our brains can clear out the daily trash. And remember, adolescents require more sleep than adults. While adults can be productive on seven hours nightly, teens need about nine and a half hours of sleep each night, even though studies show they are lucky to get seven or seven and a half hours.

As parents, our collective lifestyles may have changed since the eighties and nineties, but our children's needs remain the same. Kids desperately need to feel emotionally close to us, their parents, from the cradle until they pack their bags for college, the military, or the workforce. They also need to grow up in an intact home if at all possible. Divorce creates brokenness that, sadly, doesn't ever completely go away. I went through an unwanted divorce when my girls were young, and though they are admirable, generous, loving, and hardworking women, they would tell you that parental divorce shaped their lives in conscious and unconscious ways. If you are contemplating divorce and can pull back from the brink, do so. You will save yourself, your spouse, and your children tremendous psychological pain and likely financial strain.

In sum, it takes a lot of thought, sensitivity, diligence, and sacrifice to be a good parent and raise a child who is psychologically healthy, honest, hardworking, and brave. Of course, you can't wing it alone. You need God's help to do this. If you take your child to church and have a practicing faith yourself, you are giving him a priceless gift. And if your child has a genuine faith in Christ, she will be better able to face the world at age eighteen with strong core values, resilience, and inner strength.

As I sometimes say to clients as they leave my office, you can do it!

CHAPTER SIX

Our Earliest Attachments

She shone for me like the evening star. I loved her, but from a distance.

Winston Churchill, on his mother in *My Early Life*

When I first met Alison, she, an attractive lanky blonde, proceeded to tell me her story. She felt she was depressed and had many of the symptoms of major depression: fatigue, insomnia, low self-esteem, and lack of pleasure in life. She was unhappy at work and felt emotionally disconnected from her current husband (she had been married once before). She did not have children, nor did she want any. Her childhood had been punctuated with a painful and conflictual relationship with her father. She wondered if her family of origin—her earliest attachment relationships with her parents—had affected her marriages and her capacity for intimacy.

John called, saying he felt "stuck" in his life and wanted to come for therapy to discuss this. In his forties and divorced, John was involved with an older woman who berated and belittled him often and failed to support his dreams and aspirations. He stayed in the relationship, though he didn't understand why, and the longer he stayed, the more depressed he felt. After I asked him some questions, he revealed that his stepfather had been abusive and his mother severely depressed.

Our earliest attachments shape us. When clients come seeking help with their anxiety and depression, most do not see any connection between their emotional bonds with their parents in childhood and their current difficulties with relationships, self-image, or mood disorders. Yet it is in our families of origin and, in particular, our relationships with the first people we ever loved or tried to love—our parents—that many of our current problems lie. To understand the depressive in your life, you need to listen to his story, understand his earliest attachments to Mom and Dad, and begin to unravel how his past affects his present. As Shakespeare says in *The Tempest*, "What's past is prologue."

Attachment Theory

In his 1969 book *Attachment*, the late British psychoanalyst John Bowlby writes about the centrality of our earliest emotional bonds with or attachments to parents. He is particularly concerned about a child's bond with his mother, stating that "the young child's hunger for his mother's love and presence is as great as his hunger for food" and "her absence inevitably generates a powerful sense of loss and anger."[1] Bowlby also believes that, in the first twelve months of life, every baby forms an internal working model or mental representation of the self and the larger world based on the way his parents treat him.[2] From this internal working model flows self-image and the capacity for intimacy in all later love relationships.

Bowlby believes that our capacity to create intimate emotional bonds with our major caregivers is a basic part of human nature and that even as we grow, these early bonds persist.[3]

After Bowlby, along came researcher Dr. Mary Ainsworth, who created a brief laboratory instrument called "the Strange Situation," which peers into the quality of the emotional bond that the baby has forged with his mother. Over lunch one day, Ainsworth told me that watching a twelve-month-old baby in a lab as his mother left him with a stranger, returned, and left again—this time leaving him alone—and then finally returning, was a "fascinating little drama." She felt the two separation episodes were enormously stressful for the baby, and, therefore, the two reunion episodes provided a window into the mother-baby attachment relationship. As a grad student at Georgetown, I did a pilot study on patterns of attachment and watched videos of the babies as they experienced these stressful separations and reunions with their mothers. Their responses were incredibly different—some babies howled, and others acted like nothing significant was happening. I was an emotional wreck after three days of listening to heartrending cries.

From her early work, Ainsworth and her colleagues identified three patterns of attachment in twelve- to eighteen-month-old babies: secure, anxious resistant, and anxious avoidant. The securely attached babies had mothers who were sensitive, consistent, and responsive to their needs.[4] The babies identified as anxious resistant, on the other hand, had learned early on that they could not count on their mothers to meet their needs consistently. Sometimes the mothers did; other times they didn't. For those babies, it was like the little song children chant as they pull petals off the daisies: *She loves me, she loves me not.* Finally, the third pattern of attachment, the anxious avoidant or ambivalent, is saddest of all. Bowlby writes that this child becomes an individual who "attempts to live his life without the love and support of others" and "tries to become emotionally self-sufficient and may later be diagnosed as narcissistic or as having a false sense of self."[5] Moreover, anxious avoidant babies had mothers who rebuffed them repeatedly when they came to them seeking love and physical comfort. A later pattern of disoriented and disorganized behavior was identified in infants who had been physically or sexually abused or whose mothers were in mourning.[6]

The Strange Situation has also been used to identify the child's relationship with her father, and it was discovered that a baby could be securely attached to one parent and not the other, insecurely attached to both, or securely attached to both.

Why this foray into attachment theory? Researchers have found that attachment patterns are remarkably stable over time and even across generations. In other words, as babies, we got on a developmental path in terms of emotional security/insecurity that has influenced us ever since. Our sense of self-worth and our capacity to be close to those we love have been influenced by the way our parents treated us from infancy on. Moreover, these earliest attachments also affected our ability to trust another with our vulnerable self.

Attachment and Depression

What, you might ask, does this have to do with depression? When I take the history of a client who comes into my office complaining of depression, it soon becomes obvious that he failed to establish warm, affectionate ties with both parents in childhood. He may have been emotionally close to one parent but not the other. Or perhaps he never felt close to either parent. Sometimes he experienced trauma, such as sexual or physical abuse; sometimes he had parents who were lost in the world of alcohol or substance abuse. Sometimes his parents were absent or emotionally unavailable. Perhaps you or your loved one had parents who were overtly functional, but because of their own attachment histories, they were unable to show love, warmth, and affection.

Our earliest attachments affect us profoundly and are usually persistent. Why is this so? Bowlby writes,

> One reason for this is that the way a parent treats a child, whether for better or for worse, tends to continue unchanged. Another is that each pattern tends to be self-perpetuating. Thus, a secure child is a happier and more rewarding child to care for and also is less demanding than an anxious one. An anxious ambivalent child is apt to be whiny and clinging; whilst an anxious avoidant child keeps his distance and is prone to bully other children. In both of these last cases the child's behavior is likely to elicit an unfavorable response from the parent so that vicious cycles develop.[7]

But how is our childhood experience related to depression later in life? Bowlby suggests that the future depressive feels unable to create and maintain warm, loving bonds. He is likely to have had "a bitter experience of never having a stable and secure relationship with his parents despite having made many repeated attempts to do so, including having done his utmost to fulfill their demands and perhaps also the unrealistic expectations they may have had of him."[8] Bowlby writes, "He may have been told repeatedly how unlovable, and/or how inadequate, and/or how incompetent he is. Were he to have had these experiences they would result in his developing a model of himself as unlovable and unwanted, and a model of attachment figures as likely to be unavailable, or rejecting, or punitive. Whenever such a person suffers adversity, therefore, so far from expecting others to be helpful he expects them to be hostile and rejecting."[9] Bowlby believed, then, that a depressive's earliest attachments accounted for his feelings of helplessness, abandonment, and self-loathing.

The consequences of being unable to establish a secure bond with parents early in life are far-reaching. When a depressive experiences a job loss or financial setback, he will most likely interpret the loss as the result of something intrinsically wrong with him. He will internalize the setback or failure as *his* problem and feel devastated because he cannot fix it. The securely attached, on the other hand, is like the resilient young man who was laid off from work and, after about twenty-four hours of discouragement, was able to begin utilizing his network of friends and colleagues to search for a new job.

Bowlby once said at an American Psychiatric convention where he received the Adolf Meyer Award for lifetime achievement in psychiatric research that only the securely attached are truly resilient.[10]

Do you begin to get a sense of how painful life can be for the depressive who may have failed to develop a warm, loving relationship with either parent? These earliest attachment relationships, then, are a setup for the feelings of failure and even self-hatred so many experience in the midst of a full-blown depression. Not only does our attachment history give us a sense that we are worthy of love or that we are worthless, but it also gives us core ideas about ourselves, our capacity for intimacy, and what we can expect from others.

What Helps?

Although decades of research indicate that our earliest attachment patterns with our parents are remarkably stable, it is possible to work through our pain, unearth our core beliefs (which are out of sight and out of mind), and experience greater inner healing and freedom. As mental health providers often say, "What we don't work out, we act out." When I quote this to clients, most give a quick nod of recognition. Some of them realize that they have been acting out pain and early trauma in their intimate relationships for years.

Therapy, then, becomes the process of working it out. We examine our earliest attachments in a safe place; we give voice to pain that has been hidden but acted out. We acknowledge our anger toward others and perhaps at God. And if we can eventually forgive, we move toward greater wholeness and well-being.

Have the Depressive Tell You His Story

I have gone to some lengths to talk about our earliest patterns of attachment because studies show they affect our romantic relationships as well as our relationships with our children. When I work with couples who have been unable to establish emotional and sexual intimacy in their marriages, I often find the same pattern of emotional distance in their relationship with one or both parents.

How can you help? Ask the depressed person to tell you his story. Did he feel safe with his mother? His father? Were his parents warm, affectionate, and emotionally available? Did they say hurtful things to him?

As he answers, however haltingly, stay connected. Listen. Ah, there's such power in simply listening. Don't rush in to try to heal his hurts or to fix him. I have a question that tells me worlds about the attachment relationship my client had with his parents. I ask, "Who comforted you as a child?" All too often, the depressive will say, "No one," implying that his has been a comfortless world. If this is the case, now is the time to offer comfort, love, and understanding and to help him begin to rewrite his history, because sometimes we are lucky enough to find someone who can supply what we never received from our parents.

Mrs. Everest

I want to end this chapter on a positive note by looking at the life of a famous depressive who did not have a secure attachment with either parent, yet he changed world history: Winston Churchill. Churchill's mother, Jennie, was a socialite who had "scores of lovers," including the Prince of Wales, and was seldom present in her son's early life. Boris Johnson, the UK foreign secretary, writes in his book *The Churchill Factor: How One Man Made History* that Churchill's letters to his mother from boarding school were "full of plaintive entreaties for love, money and visits."[11] His father, who died of syphilis as a result of his promiscuous lifestyle, wrote cruel letters to his son, prophesying that he would "become a mere social wastrel, one of the hundreds of public school failures" and would "degenerate into a shabby, unhappy and futile existence." He said his son was "a young stupid" and "definitely not to be trusted."[12]

So how did Churchill become so fully human? It was Mrs. Everest, his nanny, "who gave Churchill the unstinting love he craved."[13] It was Mrs. Everest who showed up at Speech Day at Harrow when neither parent was willing to come. It was Mrs. Everest who molded his character ("Be a good Gentleman, upright, honest, just, kind and altogether lovely," adding, "My sweet old darling, how I do love you, be good for my sake.") Churchill said of her, "My nurse was my confidante. Mrs. Everest it was who looked after me and tended to all my wants. It was to her I poured out my many troubles."[14] And when she lay dying, it was Churchill who left school and rushed to be by her side, taking care of all her funeral arrangements and costs. As Johnson notes, at the time of Mrs. Everest's death, Churchill was only twenty years old.[15]

We only need to love and be loved well by one person as we grow up. Churchill was fortunate that Mrs. Everest was the surrogate mother he and his brother, John, so desperately needed. And he was also blessed in his marriage to his "Darling Clementine," who made his wishes, needs, and desires paramount during their entire marriage. While both had parents who were "serially unfaithful" and both had grown up in unhappy households, the evidence is that they loved each other faithfully and deeply.

Johnson says that Churchill could never have been the great man and leader of Britain that he was without Clementine. He writes, "She curbed his excesses, she made him think more of other people, and to be less self-centered, and she helped to bring out what was lovable and admirable in his character. That was important, in 1940. The country needed a leader the public could understand, and who was likable, and who seemed wholly 'grounded and authentic.'"[16]

So our earliest attachments matter. They shape us in ways we cannot imagine. And if we do not have parents who love us deeply and well, we may be fortunate enough to find others who love us in childhood and beyond.

CHAPTER SEVEN

Working It Out

Perfection is man's ultimate illusion. It simply doesn't exist in the universe. If you are a perfectionist, you are guaranteed to be a loser whatever you do.
David Burns, *Feeling Good: The New Mood Therapy*

At this point, you probably feel you have exhausted all your inner resources and done all you can for your depressed child, spouse, or parent. You may just feel exhausted! If you have reached this point, now is the time to have your loved one evaluated by a psychiatrist to see if he is suffering from a major mood disorder. The psychiatrist may prescribe an antidepressant if he deems it necessary. Even if your loved one starts taking an antidepressant, it is important that he begin talk therapy at the same time to address the areas of his life responsible for his depression. Otherwise, when he stops taking the drug, the same issues may be present that brought on the depression in the first place. Talk therapy can be enormously helpful and even lifesaving in dealing with depression. Why is this the case? Dr. David Burns says in his book *Feeling Good: The New Mood Therapy*, "Nearly all depressed people are convinced that they are facing some special, awful truth about themselves and the world and that their terrible feelings are absolutely realistic and inevitable."[1]

A good therapist will help expunge these feelings by making the client aware of her negative self-talk while encouraging her to change some of her core beliefs about herself. As a client learns to change the way she sees herself, others, and her world, she will begin to feel better, and the darkness will begin to lift. She is no longer a victim of her early life or her current circumstances, nor is she a pawn in the universe who is being denied the good things of life. When she gives up seeing herself as a victim and understands she is making choices daily—some good, some bad—her self-esteem will improve as well. As Burns states, "You can learn to change the way you think about things, and you can also change your basic values and beliefs. And when you do, you will often experience profound and lasting changes in your mood, outlook, and productivity."[2]

So how does talk therapy work? When a client sits down on the couch in my office, I congratulate him for seeking help. It takes courage, mixed with some desperation, to come for therapy, particularly if this is his first time or if he is male. Females are generally more comfortable discussing their feelings and past history, even if they have never thought about how the past influences the present. I generally tell them that depression is like a three-legged stool; one leg stands for *helplessness*, another for *hopelessness*, and the final leg for *hostility*. Helpless, hopeless, and hostile—these are the three *H*s of depression, as psychologists often call them. After checking the client for hopelessness—always a red flag for therapists—I ask about his current life (causes of stress, disappointments, losses, and intimate relationships with others). It's often in the relationship area that the greatest pain and hostility exist, and it is often the impetus for seeking therapeutic help.

Sometimes people like you, dear reader, seek help in dealing with the depressed person in your life who is negative, rejects your help, and frightens you with the level of darkness she emanates. But more often, it is the depressives themselves who sit on the couch, talking about where they are in their lives. Some are taking antidepressants already prescribed by their primary physicians; others say from the beginning that they do not want to take drugs. Some clients have strong feelings about not taking drugs, and if they are mildly depressed and committed to talk therapy, I will work with the client's personal choice. However, if the client has a history of depression or is severely depressed, I refer her to a psychiatrist for an evaluation and antidepressant.

Eventually, the client and I talk about lifestyle: How much sleep does he get? How nutritious is his diet? How many hours does he work each week? Sometimes clients come in complaining of low energy, and I later find they have heavy work schedules, lack uninterrupted sleep, seldom exercise, and subsist on a junk-food diet. They seem oblivious to the effects their current lifestyle has on how they feel, though it's clear their lifestyle choices are hurting and not helping them. When they begin to exercise, move toward a plant-based diet, try to get more sleep, and examine their attitudes toward work—creating a better work-life balance—they often begin to have more energy to tackle their emotional and relationship problems. And if they are drinking too much, this must be addressed and dealt with. Alcohol masks concerns (worries, fears, low self-esteem, loneliness) that need to be addressed, and if the client is an alcoholic or is alcohol dependent, I generally refer him or her to an addiction specialist.

Most will begin making lifestyle changes, one small step at a time. Since one of the symptoms of depression is "do nothingism," patience is the name of the game. As the client begins to have more energy—she's eating a bit better and getting some exercise—we start our work in earnest. Then the hurt begins to spill out as she speaks of her low self-worth, the people who have hurt her, and her excruciating disappointments. Her concerns of never measuring up, of letting others down. Her scars. Her fresh wounds. Her low mood.

As the angst pours out, I listen and work to help the depressive with his thoughts of perfectionism and the messages he received from parents growing up: that he had to be first in academics or in sports or in music. The area of achievement changes; the parental message seldom does. *Always first.* Often, depressed clients grow up with high parental expectations but little parental warmth and affection, so they drive themselves relentlessly and feel nothing they do is ever good enough. Many believe erroneously that achievement is the key to happiness and love, but when they do achieve—and sometimes have smashing successes—they still feel empty inside. Success always demands an encore. Or as one client said, "Success is a black hole."

As the client makes lifestyle changes—one small change at a time—and as she begins to process her pain and depressive thoughts in a safe place, she usually begins to feel better. She is no longer a victim of her dark moods; she can begin to work with her therapist, take charge of her negative thinking, and create positive motion in her life.

Cognitive Behavioral Therapy

One of the most effective approaches to overcoming depression is found in cognitive behavioral therapy, which addresses the way we think when we are depressed. In *Feeling Good*, Burns writes about this "clinically proven, drug-free treatment for depression from the University of Pennsylvania School of Medicine." This book has a basic, liberating premise: we feel the way we think. According to Burns, "Every bad feeling you have is the result of your distorted negative thinking."[3] He continues, "Intense negative thinking always accompanies a depressive episode, or any painful emotion for that matter."[4]

Burns advises, "Every time you feel depressed about something, try to identify a corresponding negative thought you had just prior to and during the depression. Because these thoughts have actually created your bad mood, by learning to restructure them, you can change your mood."[5]

Burns admits that the depressed person may feel skeptical about this because his negative thinking is as automatic as breathing—so automatic, in fact, that he may not even recognize it. It is as if a little creature is sitting on his shoulder saying things like "You'll never amount to much," "You don't deserve love," or "You don't have any real friends." If we are depressed, we hear this negative rant and come to believe it. Sometimes clients have an aha moment when they begin to recognize their negative thinking in therapy and then come to understand just how pervasive it is. It feels so normal. Of course, those of you who have someone in your life who thinks like this know just how debilitating it is to listen to this barrage of negativism day in and day out. You may find yourself sinking into a low mood yourself, knowing that no matter what you say, the depressive will shoot you down. And that's because he feels that his problems will not go away or be easily fixed. As David Burns says,

"Nearly every depressed person seems convinced beyond all rhyme or reason that he or she is the special one who really is beyond hope." Burns adds that this kind of thinking is at the very heart of this particular mental illness.[6]

So what helps the depressed person feel better? He must learn to identify his automatic negative thoughts, write them down, and talk back to them in a rational way. In the process, he will begin to disbelieve them and eventually expunge them. To help the depressive identify his automatic negative thinking, Burns has a list of what he calls cognitive distortions, believing that automatic negative thinking falls into one of these categories. Here are some of Burns's cognitive distortions:

- *All-or-nothing thinking.* This refers to seeing things as black or white and feeling like a total failure if you make a misstep. This kind of thinking is at the root of perfectionism and will cause you to see yourself as a "loser," "inadequate," and "worthless."[7]
- *Overgeneralization.* This occurs when a single negative event becomes an indelible pattern of defeat; for example, when a woman declines a date, a man assumes all other women will do the same.
- *Mental filter.* This refers to obsessing about a single negative event and letting it color all others; the depressed person filters out the positive and blows up the negative until everything she or he sees is negative. Burns says this is "reverse alchemy," a deliberate attempt to "transform golden joy into emotional lead."

- *Jumping to conclusions.* This refers to a kind of thinking
  where, no matter what the facts are, you jump to a negative conclusion. For example, upon hearing a diagnosis
  of depression, the depressive thinks he will be depressed
  forever.

The list also includes emotional reasoning (assuming that whatever emotion you feel is your reality) and personalization (assuming you are responsible for a negative event when you had nothing
to do with it), among others.[8] I have not included all the items on
Burns's list, so it will be helpful for you and the depressed person in
your life to have this book handy and reproduce the list, working
to eradicate negative thinking with rational responses.

The Downhill Slide

One of the images I use with clients is what I call the downhill
slide. When you start to feel depressed, imagine you are a child
again, at the playground, climbing the steps of the tallest slide.
At the top of the slide, you look down and see a big patch of wet,
gooey mud. You know that if you go down the slide, you will soon
be covered with mud and that will be a gross, unpleasant experience. So you backtrack. It's the same with depressive, negative
thinking. You begin to listen to your automatic negative thoughts
as you ascend the stairs. Then at the top, you realize what you are
doing and decide to change course. You begin to descend the stairs,
becoming acutely aware of the negative thoughts you entertained
as you ascended. If you are familiar with Burns's list of cognitive
distortions, you match them to your thoughts. In other words, you

talk back to your negative thinking, and your emotions begin to change. You catch yourself on the downhill slide before you sail to the bottom and are covered with mud.

Marie came to my office wondering why she had such struggles with depression. She had been raised with high expectations but little emotional warmth, and somehow her current achievements as a wife and mother gave her no pleasure, even though she had also published a book in her area of expertise. As we worked together and she talked about her earliest attachment relationships with her demanding parents, we also used Burns's cognitive distortions to help her identify her negative thinking. One day, she came for an appointment and said that the previous weekend she had felt herself sinking into a low mood. However, she caught herself, analyzed her thinking, and realized that she had been engaged in a mental filter. She had allowed a single negative event at a friend's house to spoil a whole evening, and only when she caught herself at the top of the slide did she descend the stairs, feeling better.

So cognitive therapy provides an excellent tool for both client and therapist to use in dealing with depression. In addition, it is important that the depressive builds a bond of trust with an empathic therapist who will listen to her story and help her sort things out. Each of us has a story filled with joy, good times, pain, and often sorrow. Sometimes those struggling with depression have tales to tell of parental abuse (either physical or sexual), loss, disappointment, desertion, or neglect—their very human saga. It is often empowering for clients who feel so utterly powerless to finally have a safe place to go and an empathic person to talk to who has the skills and training to help them begin to climb out of the depression pit.

At the same time, you may be the empathic person the depressive comes home to. Your love and compassion are critical to the whole process. If you can support the therapeutic process and deal with any feelings of being "left out," it becomes a winning situation for you and the person you care about. After all, his or her relationship with you—if you are a spouse or parent or adult child—is all-important. And your depressed loved one needs to feel heard, understood, and loved.

Dealing with Anger and Hostility

In working with depressed clients, if the client isn't feeling hopeless, I usually start with anger and hostility. Remember the three legs of the depression stool? While men may come feeling angry or "pissed off," women are often unaware of the depth of their anger and frustration. When they begin to tell their stories, however, it becomes obvious that old and new anger exists, coupled with old hurts. As they expose their wounds, often the anger emerges, directed at the person who hurt them. Perhaps it is the father who physically abused their mother. Or the relative who molested them. Or the mother or father who walked out. Or the husband who had an affair and left. Or the ever-critical mother who can never be pleased.

A woman approached me at a conference and said, "I am seventy years old, and my ninety-year-old mother is in a nursing home. To this day, she is critical of me, even of the color of my lipstick." I had just spoken on the mother-daughter relationship, so I replied, "With your genes, you may live to be ninety or even one hundred; I would suggest you find a warm, empathic therapist who can help you deal with your pain and your critical mother."

It is imperative that we deal with any unresolved anger, bitterness, and resentment. Sometimes clients feel they are betraying Mom and Dad if they share intimate tales of their painful life growing up. Often they make allowances for their abusive father or sexually adventurous brother because time has passed and they tell themselves these people have changed. However, it is important to finally tell the truth about past events and share personal and family secrets in a confidential setting. As a colleague once said to me, "We're only as sick as our secrets." As clients open up and share their dark places of hurt and woe, often for the first time, their secrets are robbed of intensity and power. It is as if the secrets become defanged once they are secrets no more.

Helplessness

In addition to hostility, depressed clients often say they feel powerless, vulnerable, and helpless. After all, most do not feel like doing much, if anything. Depending on the severity of the depression, a client may complain that he works a full schedule and then lolls around on the couch on days off, or perhaps she works during the week but does little on the weekends except drink too much. Or if a client is severely depressed, he may have trouble getting out of bed in the morning. He may also feel that he goes out to confront the world without any armor or protection—some clients say they feel as if they have no skin.

It is as if the depressive has lost any real strength she ever had, and this becomes a therapeutic issue. It often comes as a surprise when a therapist listens and suggests an assertive course of action to counter the client's passivity, which is readily apparent. This passivity or helplessness usually becomes a relationship problem because the depressive's partner or spouse gets tired of this passive approach to life and wants him "to do something" or "to say something and have an opinion." "I don't know" or "It doesn't matter to me" are not helpful responses. One depressed man was in group therapy following a messy divorce when his psychiatrist asked him what he liked for dinner. The man replied, "I don't care." The psychiatrist then stated matter-of-factly, "I bet if I offered you a hot dog or a hamburger, you would have a preference." The client never forgot that moment.

It is equally powerful to find one's voice at work and in relationships. We *do* care which movie we see or which outfit we buy or where we take a summer vacation. We *do* know which foods we like to eat and which restaurant we want to go to. One tool is to say to the depressive, "On a scale of one to ten, with ten being the number that represents your most positive feelings, how much do you want to go to this particular movie? Give me the first number that comes to mind." This can be an effective shortcut for those who are indecisive and passive.

However, if you—as a parent, spouse, or romantic partner—are controlling, you are part of the problem. You are contributing to the passivity you say you loathe. You need to back off and wait for the depressive to express an opinion or take action. If you are controlling because of your own insecurities and anxieties, then you need to address these and seek help for yourself. The more controlling you are, the more passive and indecisive the depressive may become.

Being Assertive

An antidote for the helplessness many depressives feel is asser-
tiveness. In time, as the depression begins to abate, they may be
encouraged to deal with the difficult persons in their lives head
on. One woman in her late forties had struggled with her critical
mother all her life. As she came out of her depression, she and
her therapist worked on ways to handle this "powerful'" woman
and shrink her down to human size. Together, they planned what
she would do during an upcoming visit. When the client's mother
said to her daughter, "You look awful. You really need help choosing your clothes," the daughter simply said, "Mom, we are not
going to go there. We are going to have a good visit today and
make positive comments about each other." To her surprise, her
seventy-year-old mother complied, and the visit (and the relationship) made a U-turn that day. In being assertive, the daughter felt
that she had finally found a tool she could use to deal with one of
the key players in her life. She knew she would encounter Mom's
criticism again, but she believed that if she stood her ground and
didn't become defensive or angry, she could head her mother off at
the pass. That proved to be true, and the women were finally able
to enjoy a relationship that was important to both of them.

It is healing for the depressive to find her voice. It is healing to
move from passivity to action. Sometimes, if a depressed person
will simply start to create order in her external world, she will find
that her actions affect how she feels. Cleaning a messy apartment,
straightening up a sloppy garage, or even washing the car can have
an impact. The mere act of moving the body and creating external order can have a positive effect on the internal world. One

divorced man said that it worked for him and made him feel better and more productive when he came home from work and washed the dirty dishes in the sink. Looking at chaos or disorder merely reinforces feelings of inner disarray, whereas creating external order can begin the process of healing.

Something similar happens when a client begins to write about his feelings, his earliest attachments to Mom and Dad, his wounds, and things that inspire gratitude in him. Journaling is a magnificent way of increasing self-awareness and making thoughts more real. Clients say that journaling is enormously helpful to them. They like reading what they have written aloud to me, and we discuss what they have said. They often feel they are finally unpacking the pain and trauma that have dogged their steps for years. Writing brings order out of internal chaos.

Many famous writers who had painful childhoods have written books and poetry, using their memories as writer's capital while processing pain from their early years. For example, Virginia Woolf, author of *Mrs. Dalloway* and *To the Lighthouse*, wrote about the sexual abuse she and her sister Vanessa experienced at the hands of their half brothers, George and Gerald Duckworth, in *A Sketch of the Past*. Although this famous twentieth-century British writer experienced several severe depressive episodes and ultimately committed suicide, it may be that her prodigious writing kept her alive for as long as she chose to live.

Final Thoughts

Both you and the depressed person in your life need to be prepared for the time and commitment needed to come out of a serious depression. It may take months or longer to resolve a clinical depression. And you, as a key player in your loved one's life, need to be okay with this. It takes effort to eradicate negative thoughts, to change core beliefs about the self, to process old hurts, and to understand how one's attachment history influences the present. But doing the necessary internal work can change the rest of the depressed person's life and possibly stave off a recurrent depression.

Your role is critical. Remember that you are vitally important in the depressive's life. She needs you to think well of her and encourage her to seek help. She needs you to believe that life will get better. While you may feel at times that you want to detach or run away, stay connected. When the mother of a depressed teenager said she felt like giving up, I told her, "Imagine that you and she are each holding onto the end of a rope, and both of you are pulling at the same time. Don't let go or she will fall and hurt herself." Years later, the mother said to me with a smile, "I didn't let go of the rope." When I looked at her quizzically, she reminded me of the counsel I had given and added that her daughter is today a young adult, managing her life with creativity and grace.

Don't let go of the rope. Seek help for yourself if you need it. Imagine a better future for you and for the depressed loved one in your life. Work it out.

CHAPTER EIGHT

Finding Community

The person who loves their dream of community will destroy community,
but the person who loves those around him will create community.

Dietrich Bonhoeffer, *Life Together*

Years ago, when my first husband, a psychiatric resident at Yale, had an affair with a nurse and my marriage lay in ruins at my feet, I was living with two little daughters, ages one and three, in a suburb in Connecticut. I was anxious, lonely, and depressed. Needing money, I found a job teaching English at a local high school and dropped my girls off at day care each morning. With no family nearby and no church community to support me (my pastor was uncomfortable with my marital situation), I felt desolate at times. Then a friend sent me Edith Schaeffer's *L'Abri*, a book about the ministry by the same name that the author and her husband, Francis, had created in Huémoz, Switzerland, to share their Christian worldview with university students from all over Europe. I was drawn to L'Abri and wrote the Schaeffers, asking if I could come to Switzerland. One of their daughters wrote back, encouraging me to go to London instead because the Holy Spirit was bringing Christians from all over the world to live in community around 52 Cleveland Road, the site of the London L'Abri. Within months, the girls and I were at John F. Kennedy International Airport, waiting for our plane to take off. I had quit my job and sold our house with all its furniture. With all my bridges burned, there was no turning back.

Those two years in London, living in community, were among the happiest of my life. I was no longer lonely; I had friends at the small L'Abri house church who cared about me and my children. We shared meals, rides, and housing, and we learned firsthand what Christian community feels like. They provided child care and emotional support when I had to fly back to America for a messy divorce. Over forty years later, the friendships formed then are vital, having become some of the richest relationships of my life.

Hardwired for Community

We are hardwired for community. All of us need a tribe of friends and family who see us regularly, call, and show they care about our well-being. When we have a flourishing tribe, we feel peaceful, connected, at ease … normal. When we do not, we may lapse into loneliness, isolation, and depression.

In his book *Tribe: On Homecoming and Belonging*, Sebastian Junger defines a tribe as "the people you feel compelled to share the last of your food with."[1] Junger points out Ben Franklin's observation that white people who were ransomed from Native American tribes invariably ran away to rejoin the Indians. Franklin wrote, "Tho' ransomed by their friends, and treated with all imaginable tenderness to prevail with them to stay among the English, yet in a short time they become disgusted with our manner of life … and take the first good opportunity of escaping again into the woods."[2]

"Our manner of life." If white people ran away from American society then, what does that say about our society now? Junger's main focus in his book is on war veterans who develop post-traumatic stress disorder when they leave the intimacy and comradery of the platoon and return home to a society full of disconnected people. "The assumption is that our wonderful society is good for our mental health. And the fact that it's not is shocking and also a relief to find out," Junger said in a *Time* magazine interview. "Why [else] would suicide rates go up with wealth? Why would depression go up with modernity?"[3] Junger believes that financial independence can lead to isolation and that "isolation can put people at a greatly increased risk of suicide and depression."[4]

In *Tribe*, Junger quotes anthropologist Sharon Abramowitz, who says, "You'll have to be prepared to say that we are not a good society—that we are an antihuman society. … We are not good to each other. Our tribalism is to an extremely narrow group of people: our children, our spouse, maybe our parents. Our society is alienating, technical, cold, and mystifying. Our fundamental desire, as human beings, is to be close to others, and our society does not allow that."[5]

When depressed people come for therapy, most complain of loneliness and a lack of human connection. When asked, most have few, if any, people they see outside of work. They speak of longing for companionship, and many single women believe that what they need most is a man. They believe finding the right man will lift them out of their depressive feelings and supply magical human warmth and contact that will heal all wounds. Some have no group, club, organization, or church connection; often, all they have is a job. That means they usually spend weekends alone unless they are meeting people online. For singles in this culture, finding the right partner can become an obsession. But even married couples may have few friends they see with any regularity.

Your Friendship List

What about you? Do you have close friends or family members you talk to regularly? Will they reach out to you or to your depressed child or spouse to offer a warm, friendly hand? It can be lifesaving to have these intimate connections to help us get through the inevitable hard times we all must face.

Depressed clients often say that they are so afraid of rejection that they seldom reach out. Their negative self-talk convinces them that they have failed somehow to please their unseen audience. If they do tentatively reach out and are turned down, they personalize the friend's response, thinking that they have done something to offend the other person or that they're just not good company. Clients sometimes erect large barriers in the friendship arena. Most people, I tell them, are pretty self-absorbed, and if you just ask them about themselves, you will always have someone to talk to. Of course, what nourishes the soul is that close friend who does care about what we think and how we feel—that friend who gives us equal time and doesn't talk incessantly about herself. But we have to make close friends; they do not suddenly appear.

In *Getting the Love You Want*, author and psychologist Harville Hendrix relates a dialogue about friendship that he had with a client he calls "Walter." The client came to his office looking morose and told the therapist he had no friends. Hendrix was sympathetic and said, "You must be very sad. It's lonely not having any friends."[6] Then Hendrix continued relentlessly, "There are no friends out there." Hendrix went on to explain that the world consists of strangers and if Walter wanted to have a friend, he would have to make one. In other words, he would have to do the hard work of turning strangers into friends.[7]

At all stages of human development, we will need to turn strangers into friends. When we leave college, marry, or move to a different locale, the task is always to find those individuals who can become friends. And sometimes, we have to give up our rigid ideas of what constitutes a likely friend. One client, a mother at home who was isolated and depressed, felt she could not possibly be friends with her fifty-year-old neighbor; after all, she was only thirty, and what did they have in common anyway? But after some encouragement, she reached out to the older woman, and after a while, their age difference melted away, and they became fast friends, seeing each other regularly for a cup of afternoon tea and conversation.

Working at Assembling the Tribe

Sometimes people come into our lives, and we have to expend little effort to keep them close. At other times, we have to work at reaching out, setting up social engagements, having meals together, and staying in touch with old friends from earlier years. It takes physical and emotional energy to arrange times to be with friends and to help each other out when needed. That is simply the price of friendship.

If you live with a depressed husband or wife, then you will need to be the social secretary who makes the calls and sets up time to be with others. If calling individuals is too daunting, find groups that come together because of mutual interests; some cities have meet-up groups that form around book clubs, museum outings, or gourmet cooking. Churches usually have small groups that meet in homes that encourage Christian community. Start with groups that meet regularly and then make the effort to see others for coffee or a meal together. Your depressed partner may not be able to reach out; he will personalize people turning down invitations as rejection until he understands that, according to Dr. David Burns's analysis in *Feeling Good: The New Mood Therapy*, personalization is just a cognitive distortion.[8] So it falls to you to help the depressed person in your life spend time with others. If you can extend the hand of friendship to another and keep good people in your life, both you and your depressed loved one will profit. You will be happier, and it will help her better deal with her depression.

Those Long-Term Friendships

Four women meet at a restaurant for three hours in Potomac, Maryland. They are not young women; they have been friends for twenty-two years. The youngest is soon to celebrate her seventieth birthday, the same month the oldest will be eighty. Although they now live in different states, for years they used to meet every Monday morning at a diner where they helped each other work through depression, marital issues, their difficult mothers, cancer, and the death of a spouse. They are ruggedly honest and vulnerable with each other. They guard each other's secrets. When one of the four had breast cancer, the biggest vase of flowers she received while in the hospital came from these three friends. When she was sixty-five, they gave her a necklace with four circles intertwined to celebrate their foursome. She insisted each receive the same necklace that year to wear when they came together. They say "Stop it" when they witness self-destructive behavior in each other or feel that one of them is going down rabbit trails. They try to meet each year for a retreat just to catch up with each other's lives and laugh together. They used to talk about menopause; now they talk about growing old.

Seasoned and loyal, these wise older women proclaim they are friends to the end. They have a shared history and carry each other's stories in their hearts and minds.

Keep in Touch with Friends throughout Life

It is important to keep your old friends as you make new ones. Those friends from elementary school, high school and college, early marriage, and beyond carry your personal history in their hearts and minds. Of course, it takes effort to keep in touch, to go to high school and college reunions, to remember some birthdays, to arrange girlfriend retreats, or to hike the Appalachian Trail with buddies. I encourage clients coming out of depression to keep in touch with those old friends who meant so much to them at one time because they often have few friends in their current lives. Clients will often come back from a trip or a reunion reveling in the warmth of renewed friendships. They no longer feel isolated; they have more psychic energy, and over time, this begins to help them connect in their churches, schools, or places of work in their current locales.

June Cassidy, whose story was mentioned in Chapter One, felt that her husband's golf buddies helped him come out of a clinical depression years ago. When two of the best people in his business resigned, her husband, Frank, felt betrayed. He had insomnia, gained weight, and couldn't get out of bed in the morning; eventually, he had a heart attack. "He finally went on Lexapro, and that helped him," says June, "and he also went for talk therapy. But what really helped was the golf intervention his friends staged for him. It was winter, and the group flew to Santa Domingo. Just five guys together to talk about their lives. Several even had heart disease. After a day of golf, the guys would sit around and talk about their feelings, their marriages, their health problems, their work. The group leader was Greek, and he was comfortable talking about his feelings, so he was able to help the other men open up and share their emotions."

This story illustrates how important friends can be at a time of crisis. June said that she had tried to help Frank and became frustrated and angry in the process. She welcomed his friends' intervention because the golf trip "opened Frank's eyes to the fact that he was not alone. Basically, it normalized his feelings." He was just one of the guys.

We Are the Church

If we are hardwired to need a tribe, to long for intimate connections, then this is because God made us this way. He created us not only to have an intimate relationship with Him but to have intimacy with other humans as well. And even if our parents failed to forge secure emotional bonds with us, we have another chance at intimate attachments in God's family. Other people of faith can mother us or father us, befriend us, and extend to us the compassion, sensitivity, and consistency we may have missed growing up. Other believers can give us that sense of belonging that we yearn for.

As Christians, we belong to each other and to Christ's church. In his classic little book *Life Together*, the German theologian Dietrich Bonhoeffer writes, "The physical presence of other Christians is a source of incomparable joy and strength to the believer. Longingly, the imprisoned apostle Paul calls his 'dearly beloved son in the faith,' Timothy, to come to him in prison in the last days of his life; he would see him again and have him near."[9] Remember that Timothy did not have a living father but was raised by a mother and grandmother. Bonhoeffer continues, "The believer feels no shame, as though he were still living too much in the flesh, when he yearns for the physical presence of other Christians."[10]

Bonhoeffer, who pastored the underground church in Germany during the years that Hitler was in power, believed that the prisoner, the one struggling with illness, and the Christian in exile all see physical evidence of God's love in the presence of other Christians. But, says Bonhoeffer, such fellowship is not a given, nor is it guaranteed. It is a gift of grace from God at a particular time in life. He writes, "It is grace, nothing but grace, that we are allowed to live in community with Christian brethren."[11]

Bonhoeffer believes that "we belong to one another only through and in Jesus Christ."[12] Since this is so, we need to be a part of Christ's physical, as well as his mystical, church. Scripture is clear: we are not to forsake getting together, no matter how busy we say we are or how disenchanted we have become with the church. Since no church is flawless, it takes time to feel connected, form friendships, and find a way to serve. But nothing rivals the church in what it provides: it offers worship, teaching, and a sense of meaning and purpose, as well as small groups where we can share our troubles, make new friends, and pray together.

When Ann found out she had heart disease, she and her husband joined a local Baptist church in the new city where they had moved. They sang in the choir—not because they had good voices but because the choir director invited all who wanted to praise God to join. Though Ann had a small voice, she found herself standing between two women with lilting, strong soprano voices. On several occasions, individuals prayed for her healing, and as she listened to their sweet, faith-filled prayers, she did not feel so alone. She found those five years in that church a nourishing time, and twenty years later, she remembers how people prayed for her healing and how even strangers embraced her. Those powerful hugs from women far bigger than she lifted her spirits, lessened her anxiety, and helped her deal with her diminished health and the terrifying heart attack she experienced.

As a therapist who is a Christian, I have found that those who have no faith and no church are often bereft when they are depressed. They need to increase their sources of social support, so these clients sometimes try bars, book stores, online dating, or meet-up groups—and often come up empty. Christian clients, on the other hand, tell us that they feel better after they have gone to mass or church. The darkness, isolation, and despair momentarily lift. I encourage nonbelievers who have not been raised in the church to try it, often with positive results.

But what if you or the depressed person in your life feels alienated from the church because of personal history? Perhaps you were wounded by someone's vicious tongue, or you asked for help and none came, or you felt rejected when you tried to join a closed small group. If this is true for you or your loved one, I would suggest you speak to a priest, pastor, or rector who is willing to listen and speak words of healing. If you have been hurt by the church, then a spokesman for the church needs to be a healing agent. At the same time, examine your own heart to see if you have held onto bitterness and refused to forgive. It is sin, ours and others', that keeps us from fellowship with our brothers and sisters and with God. Not only is confession good for the soul, but it is essential in restoring community.

Wherever you are, whatever you believe, know that you were created for intimacy and community, and so was the depressed person in your life. If he lacks the energy to reach out, you can do it for both of you. You can connect with new and old friends, pull extended family into your intimate circle, and find a church where you feel comfortable worshipping God and experiencing fellowship. What is paramount is that you do not linger in a state of isolation and loneliness. If you do, you may soon become depressed yourself.

Find or create the tribe you need to feel fully human.

CHAPTER NINE

Taking Care of Ourselves

Carve out and claim the time to care for yourself … and kindle your own fire.
Amy Ippoliti, *The Art and Business of Teaching Yoga*

When you use up your body, where will you live?
Sign outside a chiropractor's office in Asheville, North Carolina

When you are living with someone who is depressed, it is imperative that you take care of yourself. We have already established the fact that you probably feel frustrated, confused about what to do, and helpless much of the time. That equals chronic stress for as long as the depression lasts; also, you may find that you are beginning to go down the slide yourself with your negative thinking, wondering "Will she ever get well?" or "Will he get out of bed and go to work again?"

Mark, a school administrator whose wife suffered from a full-blown clinical depression, said that it was hard coming home to a wife who was sad and upset most of the time yet refused to talk about it. "She had a complete lack of motivation for anything. She didn't enjoy anything she did. I felt a keen sense of loss. I was struggling in my marriage," Mark said. This was not the marriage

Mark had envisioned when he married Jill. Then, she had been vivacious and full of life. "My greatest frustration came from wanting to fix the problem and being unable to do it," Mark explained. "One day, I woke up and realized that I had neglected myself in trying to deal with Jill's depression, and I knew I had to do something to help us both."

Self-care is important at all stages of life, but it is imperative when you are living with someone who is depressed. Some of us do resist the idea of caring for ourselves, especially if we were neglected by our parents or if role reversal occurred and we took care of a parent in childhood. In those circumstances, caretaking feels as natural as breathing. We even tell ourselves, with some self-righteousness, that it makes us feel good to take care of others. If we never had a parent who lovingly nurtured us, we may have no idea what it feels like to be cared for or to care for ourselves as adults. Neglect, in all its forms, feels familiar. If this is the case, that's all the more reason to look at your life and see what you can do to nurture yourself on a daily basis. It will, at first, feel unnatural to make sure you have what you need to maintain good physical and mental health, especially if you are worried about a depressed spouse or child. You may even feel you are being selfish or self-centered, but the truth is that you are simply trying to breathe and stay alive—to function during this difficult time. After all, someone has to get out of bed in the morning, put her feet on the floor, get dressed, get the kids off to school, and go to work.

You're not being selfish by finding ways to care for yourself. You are fighting for self-preservation. So let's talk about some ways you can engage in self-care.

Caring for Ourselves

First, you need to examine your habits and lifestyle. Are you eating a healthy diet, free of junk food and processed food? In recent years, we have learned from researchers that our bodies need whole grains, vegetables (of various colors), fruit, and small portions of high protein—meat, wild-caught fish, or tofu. We have also learned that drinking too much alcohol and smoking will ruin our bodies and shorten our lives. In working with depressed clients, I often tell them to look in their pantry and refrigerator and tell me what they see. Sometimes, the refrigerator is nearly empty or filled with soda, beer, and processed food. And their pantry is often filled with chips, cookies, canned food, or stuff in boxes that can't really be called "food." There is nothing alive in the refrigerator—no leafy greens, carrots, celery, spinach, lettuce, avocados, cauliflower, or berries. Clients are often unaware that what they put in their mouths has any effect on their sense of well-being. Most understand that diet is related to heart disease or the hormonal cancers, but few think diet affects their mood and mental health. Like most people, they have never taken courses in nutrition or had life-threatening illnesses that compelled them to revamp their diets.

What about you? What are you feeding your body? Are you eating nutritious food and avoiding food in boxes and cans as much as possible? Do you eat three meals each day, or do you skip meals and eat unhealthy snacks when you get hungry? Are you turning to comfort foods to help you deal with the depressive in your life? Do you incorporate raw, living food into your daily diet? Be rigorous in answering these questions. It helps to write down the answers and see where you need to improve. If you eat well—and that means salads, a variety of fruits, nuts, and vegetables, as well as whole grains like brown rice, quinoa, steel-cut oats, and bulgur wheat—you will find you have more energy to deal with your life. As a billboard I saw in Asheville, North Carolina, once said, "Junk in; junk out." Or to quote Hippocrates, the father of medicine, "Let food be thy medicine; let thy medicine be food." Most of us have heard or read Hippocrates's quote, but have you ever put it into practice?

In interviewing long-term cancer survivors for my book *Staying Alive: Life-Changing Strategies for Surviving Cancer*, I found that all of them had changed their diets, consciously giving their bodies more nutrients than they had previously. Junk food—including soda and sugary drinks—was out. Water and healthy teas—such as green and black tea, as well as herbal teas—were in. Some were juicing vegetables (such as carrots, chard, kale, celery, and cucumber) daily or even several times a day; others were making green smoothies in their Vitamix blenders to preserve fiber and have a drink each day that was loaded with nutrients. Some mixed a Green Super Food powder in water or orange juice every morning to start their day.

Green Super Food is a green powder that contains greens and grasses (like barley grass, wheat grass, and alfalfa grass, plus broccoli, spinach, and chlorella), as well as an antioxidant blend (carrots, beets, raspberries, and green tea). If you go to a grocery store that sells organic products, like Whole Foods, you will find a range of Green Super Foods to choose from—I like Amazing Grass's Green Super Food because it also contains an essential fatty acid (EFA) fiber blend, as well as probiotics and digestive enzymes. You can mix a scoop of daily greens with a glass of water or juice and see your energy level improve.

I suggest to clients who want to improve their diets that they start by simply adding a Green Super Food drink to their daily intake. After trying it, a man who had complained of lack of energy, depression, and apathy said, "I can sleep better now; I have more energy."

In addition to a Green Super Food, add EFAs to your diet. When I was diagnosed with heart disease and started learning about nutrition, I discovered that our bodies need to consume omega-3 fatty acids (or EFAs) regularly since our bodies do not produce them. Essential fatty acids are not only important in monitoring the integrity of our cell membranes, but they help correct prostaglandin imbalances, an important factor in maintaining a strong immune system and fighting cancer.[1]

Which foods contain omega-3 fatty acids? Cold-water fish, flaxseed, pumpkin seeds, hemp, and walnuts have EFAs that are extremely beneficial to health. Among cold-water fish, salmon, sardines, mackerel, herring, and blue fish are rich in omega-3s. If you are concerned about contaminants in fish, then fish oil supplements are a great way to go. If you want to get your EFAs from a plant source, I recommend flaxseed. I considered flaxseed a miracle food when I was recovering from breast cancer. Flaxseed contains ALA (alpha-linolenic acid), and not only does it have cardiovascular benefits (by lowering cholesterol), but as I learned from a physician at the National Institute of Health (NIH), it is a natural antidepressant.[2]

Add some ground flaxseed to your cereal or smoothie, and you will discover that your skin begins to glow and your hair has greater sheen and more volume. You will be amazed at the results. Some women have added flaxseed to their diets simply because of its positive effects on skin and hair alone, never mind its cardiovascular benefits or breast cancer–fighting powers. Your body will be grateful that you are no longer expecting it to run on fast food or dinners straight out of the box.

The Anti-inflammatory Diet

If you are looking for more guidance, Dr. Andrew Weil's antiinflammatory diet offers an excellent guide for those who want to improve their diet and, consequently, their health. Weil suggests that we consume low-glycemic carbohydrates, such as whole grains, beans, winter squashes, and sweet potatoes. As for fats, he recommends we use extra-virgin olive oil or organic canola oil, while avoiding regular safflower, sunflower, corn, and cottonseed oils. He suggests we eat less butter, cream, high-fat cheese, chicken with skin, and fatty meats. In addition, it's important to avoid margarine, vegetable shortening, and partially hydrogenated oils. Weil further suggests we include the good fats in our diet, like avocados and unsalted nuts (walnuts, cashews, and almonds), as well as nut butters made from these delicious nuts.

As for protein, Weil believes we need between 80 and 120 grams a day. He recommends that we decrease our consumption of animal protein (except for fish, natural cheese, and yogurt) and get the majority of our protein from vegetables, especially beans and soy foods. He recommends sardines, salmon (fresh, frozen, or canned), herring, and black cod—all of which are high in the essential omega-3 fatty acids. In addition, omega-3 fortified eggs, flaxseeds (freshly ground), and hemp seeds are also rich in omega-3s. Finally, he suggests fresh fruit, especially berries, for fiber, along with beans and fiber-rich cereals. For Weil's complete anti-inflammatory diet, go online to www.drweil.com. You might also subscribe to his free daily newsletter.[3]

In addition, eat more wild-caught fish to lift your mood. Dr. Joseph Hibbein, of the National Institute on Alcohol Abuse and Alcoholism, reported in the prestigious British medical magazine *Lancet* that a correlation between fish consumption and major depression exists. In other words, countries that eat more fish report less major depression, with Japan, the greatest fish consumer in the world, leading the pack. Higher blood plasma concentrations of docosahexaenoic acid, an essential fatty acid found in fish, are linked to increased serotonin turnover in the brain and a lower incidence of depression and suicide.[4] So eat more fish, particularly those high in omega-3s, to stay out of the depression pit, and encourage your partner to do the same to help him heal from his depression. But make sure the fish is caught in the wild rather than farm raised, since you get more anti-inflammatory omega-3s and less of the inflammatory omega-6s in wild-caught fish. Moreover, farm-raised fish have higher levels of cancer-causing chemicals—namely, PCBs and dioxin.[5]

Love That Exercise!

We've all heard it—those of us who are athletes and those who are couch potatoes. We need to get regular exercise. This especially applies to those who are depressed, as well as those living with a depressive. Did you know that Hippocrates said, "If you are in a bad mood, go for a walk. If you are still in a bad mood, go for another walk"? Some athletic readers may jog; others may like to amble outside in the sunshine. Dr. Larry Crawford, when asked by a heart patient how to deal with stress, answered, "Go exercise." This cardiologist at Duke practices what he tells his patients and often greets them in his jogging shoes when he does his regular assessment. Find something you like to do—dancing, biking, using a NuStep or treadmill, or simply walking daily with a friend. But remember, women do not like to walk alone. Join a women's walking group that meets weekday mornings and enjoy your female companionship as you exercise. Or if you prefer, choose a friend with whom you can be open and share your feelings. At the end of the walk, you will have helped your heart with exercise and soothed your soul by sharing.

Of Time and Space

An anxious, high-powered woman going through menopause discovered a meditation app, downloaded it, and listened to a male voice speak soothingly about "the mountain." When her anxiety level skyrockets, she feels as if her estrogen level is bouncing off the walls, and she's convinced she will lose her major clients on Monday. Then she listens to the meditation and feels her body begin to relax. What's the result of adding meditation to her life? She's sleeping better at night and has an easier time controlling her anxiety. The Internet abounds with meditation apps and soothing spa music to lower your blood pressure and help you relax.

Some of us find the early morning, when the light is breaking, to be the best time of day to read our Bibles, pray, and meditate or to listen to the still, small voice of the Holy Spirit inside us. Sitting alone in a room as sunlight begins to stream over you, you can ask God to speak to you from Scripture, and then you can sit quietly with a pen and your journal to write down what He says. This is a practice that Sarah Young, the author of the huge bestseller *Jesus Calling*, did for years before she wrote her book that millions say makes Jesus real to them.

If you establish a practice of seeking the Lord at the beginning of the day, you will find that you feel quietly centered for the rest of it, and you can then deal with whatever the day may bring. Mornings are also a time to pray earnestly and to ask God for strength, wisdom, and guidance as you deal with the depressed adult or child in your life. You might pray that your loved one's negativity and darkness do not penetrate your soul; you might also ask God what you should do to counter that universal sense of helplessness. Finally, you can pray that the depressive gets well and that her darkness lifts.

There's something beautiful about starting your day this way. You become infused with peace. You can focus on your tasks more intently. And it helps you come to eventide with a grateful heart.

The Necessity of Friendship

Whether you are male or female, dear reader, you need a friend who cares about you to support you in your current situation. It's bleak indeed to be alone with someone who is battling depression, feeling lonely and isolated. Isolation makes depression worse. Infinitely worse. And it will exacerbate your negative feelings.

Remember the words of the famous British Anglican and metaphysical poet John Donne:

> No man is an island,
> Entire of itself,
> Every man is a piece of the continent,
> A part of the Main.

We are all related and intertwined with each other. If I didn't convince you in Chapter Eight, I want to be sure you recognize the beauty and necessity of friendship now. We need friends in our lives, whether we are young or old. In 1999, the *Washington Post* published an article entitled "50 Years Later, These Girls Are Still in the Game."[6] This is an account of a group who called themselves "the Canasta Girls." Founded by Maria Lehman and Louise Parker in 1949, these women met once a month and over time became friends. They raised their children together and eventually buried their husbands. They shared lunch and news about their lives, and they grew old. Yet even at the end, they said, "We're not old ladies; we're the girls." One of my friends had a mother in that Canasta group. Always outgoing, she lived into her nineties.

If you are a woman, take a day and spend it with girlfriends. Or take a weekend trip and clear your head. This can be a wonderful tonic and a great way to strengthen your resolve to take better care of yourself. We need other women throughout our lives—cradle to grave. But what about men, who do not share feelings the way we women do? Do they need close friends as part of their self-care when they are dealing with someone who's depressed? Absolutely.

Remember Mark, the school administrator, and his depressed wife, Jill?

Mark decided he had to make some changes in his life for the sake of self-preservation. He had a male friend at work he saw sometimes, so he decided that he would ask his friend to meet him early on Friday mornings for coffee and conversation. He needed at least one person outside his marriage he could be honest with. Because of these conversations, he decided to see a psychotherapist to better understand his own feelings and learn how to deal with Jill. Moreover, he realized he had not lived his own dream of becoming an accountant but had gone down the education path his overbearing stepfather had suggested. So he resolved to sit down with a career specialist to see if he could change the direction of his work life. He took action to improve his inner and outer life.

If you are living with a depressed wife, then you need to contact your buddies and go to a baseball or basketball game, hike in the mountains, or take a fishing trip. Since men often participate in activities when they get together, plan an activity and call some friends. Reach out and engage in meaningful conversations with others. You will feel better, and your own mental health will greatly improve.

Rediscover Your Dreams

Finally, in caring for ourselves, we may need to rediscover our dreams. Sometimes when we are in crisis, we get lost in the emotions and pressures of the moment. Sometimes, we feel we have lost our way—that we have gone "astray from the straight road" and are "alone in a dark wood," as Dante said in the beginning of

The Inferno.[7] That's the time to remember that you are a unique and separate person and that you alone cannot heal the depressed person in your life, no matter how hard you try. Granted, you can be instructive, loving, and compassionate, *but you need to save some of yourself for yourself.* One way to do this is to rediscover your lost or disowned dreams and, if you can, incorporate them into your life. One woman said that, in her late thirties, she went to the beach and spent time alone, just gazing at the ocean. She was a tenured social psychologist at a prestigious university, but she felt she wanted to become a clinical psychologist and work with troubled adolescents. She knew her colleagues might not understand and might even judge her; after all, who gives up a tenured position at a top college? But she felt in her heart it was time for a change, even though she would need a year of further education. Her husband was supportive, she braved her colleagues' surprise and shock, and she started afresh in a field she has come to love.

So write the book you always wanted to write. Or start a blog. Start your own business, no matter how small. Take dance lessons. Join a book club. Find a great cookbook at the local library and cook your way through it. Take a university course to sharpen your brain or finish your college or graduate degree. Don't worry about how old you are. As a friend and colleague told me, "It doesn't matter how long it takes you to achieve a goal; what matters is that you achieve it."

In my twenties, I wanted to get my doctorate in English. So my first husband and I had a deal. I would support us by teaching English in a local high school until he had finished medical school and his internship. Then I would begin work on my degree. Sadly, our marriage ended in divorce, and for years, all my energies went into motherhood and earning enough money to keep me and my daughters afloat. Then in my forties, when I was married to Don, he encouraged me to dust off my dream.

One Sunday afternoon, he drove me to Georgetown University from our home in Virginia and said, "See how close this school is? It's a thirty-minute drive from our house. Why don't you apply?" I protested. I said I could never get into that school. Besides, I had only taken one psychology course in my undergraduate career at Wheaton.

Then something marvelous happened. Months later, I took my older daughter, Holly, to Georgetown, and while she was touring the campus, I climbed the steps of White-Gravenor Hall to the third floor and marched into the psychology office. The only professor there that Friday was Dr. Daniel Robinson, the department chair. Without an appointment, I was ushered into his office, and we talked about the doctoral program. He said the program was based on the Oxford tutorial, and since I had published books, he felt sure I would feel at home meeting weekly with my professors, working independently, and reading and writing my way through the program.

As it turned out, I was awarded my doctorate in psychology from Georgetown when I was fifty years old. I was thrilled to have achieved this dream at last. In the process, I learned a valuable truth—if we use it, the brain will not rot.

So dream on. In fact, our dreams sustain us. Often, they are God-given and are part of our destiny. Some of us were aware of our dreams in childhood or adolescence: We were often introverts and voracious readers, and we wanted to grow up to be writers. Or we made people laugh and wanted to be comedians, at least in our families. Or we longed to travel the globe and became journalists. Or we grew up in miserable families and wanted to have our own families and do better than our parents had done.

Whatever your dreams were, get in touch with them again. Resurrect them and see how they can become realities in your own life. One of my favorite poems is by the African American poet Langston Hughes; it is called "Dreams." Here is the first stanza, which I often quote to clients:

> Hold fast to dreams
> For if dreams die
> Life is a broken-winged bird
> That cannot fly.[8]

We need not be "broken-winged birds"; we were meant to fly, to soar. A favorite quote from *Walden* by Henry David Thoreau reads, "Go confidently in the direction of your dreams! Live the life you've imagined." He certainly did just that during those two years, two months, and two days at Walden Pond when he lived a simple existence close to nature, plumbing the depths of life.

If you have the courage to step out and move in the direction of your dreams, you may be amazed at the results. You will begin to feel inspired. Your self-confidence will grow. And who knows what positive impact this can have on the one you love who is struggling with depression?

Finally, I need to say this. *You cannot fix or heal the depressed person in your life.* Nor can you ultimately save him or keep him alive. In fact, no therapist or psychiatrist can keep a patient with major depression alive if he is determined to end his life. A psychiatrist can prescribe drugs and hospitalize a suicidal patient, but ultimately, the depressive has to keep himself alive. He has to choose life and work hard to banish the darkness, even if he feels apathetic and somewhat paralyzed. He has to be willing to seek professional help. He has to somehow believe the light will return and illuminate his darkened inner world. He has to believe that the God who created him loves him with an unimaginable love and will rescue him if he only asks.

So lay your burden down and take care of yourself. As you do, you will be infused with peace and a sense of well-being that will carry you through your days of trial.

CHAPTER TEN

The Way to Forgiveness

*It may be an infinitely less evil to murder a man than to refuse to forgive him.
The former is an act of a moment of passion: the latter is the heart's choice.*
George MacDonald, *George MacDonald Anthology*

Forgiveness is a trainable skill just like learning to throw a baseball.
Fred Luskin, *Forgive for Good*

When depressed clients come for therapy and begin to haltingly tell their stories, it soon becomes apparent that they have people in their lives who hurt them deeply. They rehearse the wrongs, usually with the same intensity of emotion they felt when those wrongs first occurred. They often have stored-up hurts that their parents may have knowingly or unwittingly inflicted on them when they were growing up. Sometimes they were savaged by former spouses or lovers who cheated and broke their hearts. Or they may have felt betrayed by friends who rejected them and moved on. Or they may have had years of estrangement from parents who divorced, with one parent consigning the abandoned family to poverty. What they seldom realize is that they are bound to these people in their hearts and minds by an unbreakable bond, even though the hurt was inflicted years earlier.

Stories vary. Emotional pain is a constant.

As we work on these key relationships in therapy over time, the question of forgiveness inevitably comes up. "How can I forgive my parents who pushed me mercilessly to achieve and flogged me for any perceived failure?" a thirtysomething man asks. Or "How can I forgive my alcoholic mother who was never there for me and is now throwing her life away?" an adolescent wails. "How can I forgive that friend who said she would be there for me and bailed when I needed her?" How indeed? As I help clients articulate their deep emotional and psychological pain, I understand that if they are ever going to be free, they will need to grapple with the necessity of forgiveness, as distasteful as it first appears.

Sometimes the resistance comes from a misunderstanding of what forgiveness truly is.

In his book *Forgive for Good: A Proven Prescription for Health and Happiness*, Dr. Fred Luskin, cofounder and director of the Stanford University Forgiveness Project, writes about what forgiveness is and what it is not.

According to Luskin,

- Forgiveness is for you and not the offender.
- Forgiveness is taking back your power.
- Forgiveness is taking responsibility for how you feel.
- Forgiveness is about your healing and not about the people who hurt you.
- Forgiveness helps you get control over your feelings.
- Forgiveness can improve your physical and mental health.
- Forgiveness is becoming a hero instead of a victim.

- Forgiveness is a choice.
- Everyone can learn to forgive.[1]

In discussing what forgiveness is not, Luskin suggests that forgiveness does not mean that we give up our right to feel angry, nor does it mean that we condone the harmful things we have suffered at the hands of another. Luskin adds to the list of what forgiveness is not:

- Forgiveness is not condoning unkindness.
- Forgiveness is not forgetting that something painful happened.
- Forgiveness is not denying or minimizing your hurt.
- Forgiveness does not mean reconciling with the offender.
- Forgiveness does not mean you give up having feelings.[2]

Luskin, who has conducted forgiveness workshops around the world, believes that forgiveness is a skill that can be learned by anyone, and it does not need to have religious underpinnings.

For the Christian, however, forgiveness is regarded as a necessity, and it is mandated in Scripture. In Matthew 18, Jesus tells the parable of the unforgiving servant. The parable begins with the story of a king who initially orders his servant—who owes him ten thousand talents but cannot pay his debt—to be sold along with his wife and children. Upon hearing his sentence, the servant falls to his knees and implores his master to give him time to pay the debt in full. Touched, the king forgives his debt. But then this forgiven servant goes out and finds another servant who owes him a hundred denarii. Does he forgive this man's lesser debt? Hardly. He chokes him and has him thrown into prison. Unfortunately for him, his fellow servants report his behavior to the king, who summons him immediately for an audience. Then the master-king excoriates him for his unforgiving heart and has him thrown into prison until he can pay his debt in full.

Christ ends his parable with these sobering words: "So also my heavenly Father will do to every one of you, if you do not forgive your brother from your heart."[3]

Forgiveness Isn't Cheap or Easy

How do we forgive our brother (sister, uncle, friend, boss, father, mother, spouse, or child) from the heart? Forgiveness isn't easy; there is no cheap forgiveness. For most clients, it is a struggle they don't wish to have. When we first discuss the concept in a therapy session, they will often look at it and table it for a while. They read *Forgive for Good*, sometimes one chapter at a time, and begin to absorb its message. We begin to talk about what forgiveness is and what it is not. I suggest that forgiveness is a gift we give ourselves. It is a transaction between our hearts and God. It's a vertical transaction, at least at first. And it eases our hearts immediately.

Forgiveness is not the same as reconciliation with the offender. You can obtain great psychological relief once you choose to forgive the one who hurt you even if you never speak to her about the offense. And should you choose to talk to the offender about the pain she caused you, there is no guarantee she will own the offense or even accept your forgiveness. If she does not want to forgive and reconcile, she may deny she ever did anything wrong. Even though the two of you may never achieve reconciliation, amazing relief can come when you choose to forgive.

When clients actually forgive the people they may have hated for years, sometimes their physical appearances change. One client smiled more often and had better eye contact. When he came for his first session, he sat at the far end of the comfy brown sofa in my office, huddled in his pain, untrusting, while I sat in my leather chair across the room. But over time, as he began to make peace with his past and forgive, he slowly moved down the sofa until he was sitting directly across from me.

But What about Great Wrongs?

But what if the wrong done to the depressive in your life was unbelievably cruel and even evil?

George MacDonald—the Scottish pastor who influenced C. S. Lewis, the famous twentieth-century Christian and writer of the Narnia stories—says that if we refuse to forgive another, we cannot possibly believe that God is willing or "wanting" to forgive us. He writes,

> If God said "I forgive you" to a man who hated his brother and if (as is impossible) that voice of forgiveness should reach the man, what would it mean to him? How would the man interpret it? Would it not mean to him "You may go on hating. I do not mind it. You have had great provocation and are justified in your hate"? No doubt God takes what wrong there is, and what provocation there is, into account; but the more provocation, the more excuse

that can be urged for the hate, the more reason, if possible, that the hater should be delivered from the hell of his hate.[4]

Perhaps you think that it is wrong to say that someone struggling with a clinical depression "hates" the people who wronged her. Perhaps you feel that the depressed person in your life does not "hate" anyone. But it is easy for hurt to become bitterness and quiet hatred over time. And with hatred comes an inner darkness that the depressive may not even recognize has anything to do with her bitterness and resentment. Yet that spirit of darkness begins to lift when she forgives the person who wronged her. Hence the transformations I sometimes see as clients work through their pain and come to that place of forgiveness—such as my client Karen, who has given me permission to use her story.

Karen came for counseling because she was struggling with the diagnosis of myasthenia gravis, an incurable neuromuscular disease that produces extreme muscle weakness and fatigue. A young, attractive woman who had been healthy in her early twenties, Karen began to notice muscle weakness and soon was unable to maintain her old job in accounting. Her young husband soldiered on as a middle school teacher, and they somehow managed on a single income.

She was depressed and said during her first session that she was isolated at home and had no local friends or job. She said that because of her illness, she would fall down, sometimes couldn't walk, and had little strength in her upper body. She also said that most who suffered from this disease had experienced extreme stress in their childhoods. That was Karen's situation. Later, she told me her story:

> I came to therapy a broken person. Not only was I dealing with the reality of an incurable neuromuscular disease, but I kept holding onto the things my parents had done to me growing up. My dad, who never felt loved and was abandoned by his mother, insisted that my sisters and I dress in long dresses. We were never allowed to wear short skirts or pants. We could not bring friends to our house, where we were homeschooled by my mother. As an adult, I kept holding onto the hurt my parents inflicted with their strict dress code, isolation, and impossible ideals. I was angry and depressed even before I was diagnosed.
>
> I remember when I was fourteen years old and ran away from home. When I returned days later from a friend's house, my mom sat on me as I lay on the floor and my dad beat me with a belt. They barred my windows and took off the door, and one of them slept on the floor in front of my bed for a month. During that time, I wanted to die but knew I could not kill myself. Later, when I became ill, my parents showed no compassion and felt that God was punishing me. "You're not doing the right thing," I was told. "If you were, you wouldn't be sick."

As Karen worked through her anger and deep emotional pain over the months, she began to understand her parents better. Neither had been well loved or nurtured in their parental homes: Her father admitted he had received no hugs or kisses growing up and had in fact spent several years in an orphanage after his mother abandoned him. Karen felt her mom, whose father died when she was young, was jealous of her girls because they had a father, whereas she could barely remember hers. Karen began to understand just how broken her parents were and how wounding their own early attachments had been. She realized that her parents had little to give her that was positive and life affirming. This helped her understand the origin of her negative feelings about herself—that she was never good enough and didn't fit in at home or with her Christian friends.

As Karen began to see her parents in a more realistic light, she understood that she was different from them. "I'm my own person," she said. "I'm a separate person who has her own relationship with God, and it's good." She began to differentiate herself from her parents and give up her desire for their approval. As she did so, she started to feel free and finally was able to forgive them for all the hurts they had inflicted—for being the people they were.

After dealing with these painful relationships, Karen wanted to talk about her sorrow over the fact that she didn't feel she could care for a baby. Because of her muscle weakness, she was afraid she could not lift or carry a young child. Moreover, she was on heavy doses of Prednisone, which had produced osteoporosis; she worried how the drug would affect any pregnancy. So she and her husband mourned the loss of children they felt they would never have.

During our time together, Karen was offered a job as a nanny for a toddler who could hoist himself in and out of his crib; at the same time, she and her husband acquired two dogs that she had to care for. She even found a female friend, and on Tuesdays after her therapy session, Karen and this older woman had lunch together and watched *Downton Abbey*. By the time she concluded her therapy, Karen was no longer depressed; she had made friends, her marriage was better, and she found she could work after all. She also started having visits with her parents, and those visits were no longer painful because she had realistic expectations about what she would gain from these relationships and she set healthy boundaries. She purposefully kept the visits short. Most important, she had forgiven her parents for being who they were—limited, emotionally impoverished, broken people.

When I started writing this book, I contacted Karen because I felt she had successfully come out of depression and loss—the loss of her health and the loss of her dream of ever having children. At the beginning of psychotherapy, she *was* her illness, but at the end of our time together, her illness was but part of a larger, happier life. She coped with her limitations and rejoined the world of people. Imagine my surprise when she picked up the phone and within minutes told me that she and her husband had a four-month-old son. "I have a normal, healthy baby, and I am able to hold him," she proclaimed, her voice rippling with happiness. Her disease? It was in remission. Karen sounded joyous. She felt her life had been transformed.

The Beauty of Forgiveness

Forgiveness is a hard but beautiful thing. It sets us free from the ball and chain we have been dragging through life since the time we were wounded. A middle-aged friend said that after he forgave his abusive mother and the father who had abandoned him, he found that when he woke up at night to go to the bathroom, his mind was peaceful; he no longer ruminated into the wee hours of the morning. He had learned that we can do what God has mandated: forgive those who hurt us because we have been forgiven so very much. And what a relief it is to feel that we can *will* to forgive. We don't have to wait months or even years to *feel* like forgiving the person who wronged us. Moreover, we can trust that our emotions will one day catch up with our will.

C. S. Lewis wrote about this in *Letters to an American Lady*:

You know, only a few weeks ago I realized suddenly that I at last had forgiven the cruel schoolmaster who so darkened my childhood. I'd been trying to do it for years; and like you, each time I thought I'd done it, I found, after a week or so it all had to be attempted over again. But this time I feel sure it is the real thing. And (like learning to swim or to ride a bicycle) the moment it does happen it seems so easy and you wonder why on earth you didn't do it years ago. ... I also get a quite new feeling about "If you forgive you will be forgiven." ... I don't believe it is, as it sounds, a bargain. The forgiving and the being forgiven are really the very same thing. But one is safe as long as one keeps trying.[5]

Lewis wrote these words on July 6, 1963. He died on November 22 of that same year. Years earlier, he had set his will in motion to forgive the cruel schoolmaster. And his emotions finally caught up mere months before he died.

Lewis died a free and emotionally healed man.

What about You and Your Loved One?

Do you have a person or people you need to forgive? Do you need to forgive the depressed person in your life for the pain and difficulties he creates for you? Do you have people in your past who have wounded you, but you have become so familiar with the weight of your quiet bitterness that you ignore or deny any need to forgive them? What about the friend who left your life after being your best friend for years? What about your child's failure to live up to your expectations? What about the spouse or boyfriend who cheated—and then cheated again?

You may need to sit with yourself, bringing along a notebook and a pen to jot down the names of all the people God would have you forgive. Study the names. State how they wronged you out loud, and then say out loud that you forgive these people.

Maybe you need to write down all the hurts this person caused you, put the piece of paper in a metal bowl, and go outside to burn the paper, releasing all the hurt to God. One woman found that she needed to go to her father's grave and tell him just how angry she was for the way he had controlled her life, put her down, and refused to love her. She accused; she wept. Then she finally forgave this man who caused her so much pain. She said that when she got in her car, she felt lighter and freer than she had in years. Then she, who had been an isolate, joined a church and a quilting group. She invited people into her life and was no longer so alone.

Of course, to forgive, we will have to give up the victim stance and any hidden pleasure we get out of rehearsing the wrongs. We will also have to let go of any hatred and bitterness. Remember, forgiveness is costly. Securing the forgiveness for all our ugly sins cost Christ his life. But oh, the outcome when the deed is done. Forgiveness is transformative and energizing.

With God's help and a will set in motion, all of us can forgive. To forgive or not to forgive is ultimately just a choice.

The flip side of forgiveness is to ask God if we have offended anyone. Just as we have been hurt and offended, so have we offended others. My friend Nancy used to sit with her three friends on Monday mornings, rehearsing the wrongs that her alcoholic mother had committed. And when her mother came to visit, she would act like a policewoman, making sure her mother never had a glass of wine. Her mother resented this deeply and let Nancy know it. Then one day, my friend had an epiphany. She realized it was not her job to try to control her mother's drinking, but it was her job to be a loving daughter. And so she wrote her mother a letter asking for forgiveness for her bad attitudes, controlling behavior, and judgmental stance. Her mother, who had not communicated with Nancy for months, wrote back and promptly forgave her. This simple heartfelt action radically changed the women's relationship. They started to develop a lovely mother-daughter friendship—and it is good that they did, because Momma is now ninety-nine years old!

Recently, I met with a woman who had been my best friend for eighteen years. We had a falling out after we had moved to different states and were under severe stress. Both of us felt we had to move on, but both of us suffered because of the estrangement. We spoke on the phone over the years, but I felt I had to make amends. I called my friend, and we drove miles to meet at lunch. We spoke openly about how the broken friendship had hurt us, and we made amends. At the end, my friend said, "Are we okay?" I replied, "Absolutely." And before we parted, we made plans to meet this summer, with our husbands in tow.

Forgiveness is powerful. I have seen it lift depression, change a person's physical appearance, deepen intimacy, and set people free.

No wonder I say that it's magical.

CHAPTER ELEVEN

Hold onto Hope

I remembered that the real world was wide, and that a varied field of hopes and fears, of sensations and excitements, awaited those who had courage to go forth into its expanse to seek real knowledge of life amid its perils.

Charlotte Brontë, *Jane Eyre*

As I walked into the large room filled with chairs in the Korean ambassador's light and airy home in Washington, DC, I thought about the speech I was about to give. It was the Christmas season, and the room was already filling up with well-dressed ambassadors' wives from all over the world, busily greeting each other. I had spoken to the ambassadors' wives several years before, and I enjoyed these women; they were a gracious and responsive group.

I had chosen to speak that day about hope. Christmas is, after all, the season of hope because of Christ's birth, but I had learned some important lessons about hope from the suffering in my life and particularly as I had watched a young friend battle ALS. While I had been invited to give a speech to merely celebrate the season, I knew as a psychologist that in any group of women, some would be dealing with children gone awry, anxiety and depression, homesickness, worries about their marriages and maybe their health. And in this group, some would have concerns about the stability of governments in their home countries. I took to the podium and began to speak about hope.

Hope.

What is this enduring but ephemeral attitude or feeling that can, in the case of depression, mean the difference between life and death? The *Cambridge Dictionary* says that hope is "the feeling that something desired can be had or will happen." To hope is to look to the future with some degree of expectancy. It is to believe one has a future (which depressives find hard to imagine), and if one is a Christian, even if the future is death, it is to believe in Christ and the resurrection of the body. To hope means to look ahead at the glimmer of light shining out of the gloom, banishing the darkness.

Hollywood's Version of Hope

Hollywood dealt with the theme of hope in the movie *Cast Away* (2000), the survival epic about a FedEx employee (Tom Hanks) who washes up on a deserted island after his plane crashes. Fortunately, he lives. Near the end of the film, despairing that he will ever be rescued, Hanks's character, Chuck Noland, attempts to hang himself but fails. A few days later, a piece of corrugated metal washes up on shore, and Noland uses it as a sail for the roughhewn raft that takes him out to sea, where he is ultimately rescued. After his rescue, Noland returns to Memphis and tells a friend that he is heartbroken that he has lost Kelly, his fiancée who married someone else during the four years Noland was on the island. But then Noland shares a valuable truth he learned from his failed suicide attempt. He said he realized, "I've got to keep breathing. Tomorrow, the sun will rise, and who knows what the tide will bring in?"

I've got to keep breathing. In this book, we have learned that suicide is always possible for the person suffering from a major depressive disorder. And this usually happens when he has lost hope. Hope that he will come out of the darkness. Hope that life will get better. We must have some degree of hope to endure, to keep on living. This is why it is important to track a depressive's feelings about hopelessness, for when he lapses into despair and stays in that dark and forbidding place, all the bells and whistles should go off, because all hands are needed on deck to help the depressive find his way to hope again.

While *Cast Away* provides a Hollywood version of hope, one woman found Noland's rumination enormously helpful. In the middle of a family tragedy, she made a mantra based on this movie and what her hairdresser, Tommy, said to her one day. It went like this: "It is what it is; we are where we are. Tomorrow, the sun will come up, and who knows what the tide will bring in?" This combination of acceptance and hope was comforting to her as she worked her way to a better place.

Abraham, the Father of Hope

While a movie character can offer a certain degree of hope, no one plumbs the depths of hope like Abraham, one of the most famous people in the Bible. His hope is tried decade after decade, yet he unwaveringly believes in God's promise that he will become "the father of many nations" and "heir of the world." Imagine how long Abraham waited for this magnificent promise to be fulfilled. Years flew by. He grew older until his body, at one hundred, was withered and "as good as dead." How could he, with his old wife, Sarah, have a child who would fulfill God's promise and make him this great father of nations? Then comes that heart-stopping verse in Romans: "*Against all hope*, Abraham *in hope* believed and so became the father of many nations, just as it had been said to him." It happened. Abraham's wife, Sarah, actually conceived a child in old age, and nine months later, Isaac, child of the promise, was born.[1]

Are you at the place in your life where "against all hope" you are still hoping that the person you love will find healing and wholeness in the future? Perhaps your loved one has fallen into a silent hopelessness and despair, or maybe you feel hopeless yourself about the possibility of a full recovery. If this is so, let those words "against all hope, Abraham in hope believed" seep into your very soul and comfort you. You are not alone. Many of us have found ourselves "against all hope," yet we have chosen to continue holding onto hope. In those moments, we realize that if God doesn't rescue us, we are lost. Utterly lost. He is all we have for sure.

Hope often rises out of severe emotional turmoil or physical suffering. While we may have a superficial sense of well-being that we call hopefulness when life is good, genuine hope emerges from the fire of suffering. Romans reminds us that "suffering produces perseverance; perseverance character; and character hope."[2] One day, it occurred to me, as I was buffeted by waves of fear and suffering in an attempt to deal with a life-threatening illness, that if you trace those famous words in Romans backward, you immediately see that hope is rooted and grounded in suffering. It is as we *suffer* that we learn to *endure*, and from that place of endurance, our *character* matures and deepens. Then we realize that, in spite of circumstances, we have *hope*. In fact, when we get to this point, hope is all we have.

All too often, it is only when we are confronted with profound loss, our mortality, or physical or financial ruin that we can begin to grasp what hope is and see it rise from the ashes of our broken dreams, just like the legendary bird, the phoenix. Mythology says that this ancient, beautiful firebird lived five hundred or more years only to be ignited in its nest; but then a new phoenix would emerge from its ashes with healing in its wings. A symbol for immortality and resurrection, the phoenix is synonymous with the hope that springs eternal in the human breast.

As long as we have breath, we cling to hope. When individuals attempt or succeed in killing themselves, they have lost all hope. They no longer believe that their lives will get better or that the torment of depression will lift. They simply cannot see any light in their dark night of the soul. Their minds are clouded over with negativity and depression. Their bodies may be racked with chronic pain with no end in sight. Or they may have cancer or ALS, a disease where the one with the affliction knows the end from the beginning. At that moment, we must cast ourselves on God's mercy and "hope against all hope," somehow believing that the God who loves us knows exactly where we are in the universe, even in the height of our pain and distress. He knows our address. He knows our telephone number. So we cast our despair and unbelief on God, who the Bible tells us cannot lie. Only then do we begin to realize that "we have this hope as an anchor for the soul, firm and secure."[3]

In my work with clients struggling with end-stage cancer or ALS, I have watched both believers and nonbelievers deal with periods of hopelessness. Ultimately, it is the Christian who usually emerges from despair, having gained strength and perspective from her faith and a belief system that helps her embrace hope in the face of insurmountable odds. Nonbelievers have no hope of life after death or any hope in an intimate, personal God. They may have a loving family, an accomplished career, and a sizable network of supportive friends, but ahead is all darkness and the unknown. Some consider suicide. Christians, on the other hand, who believe in heaven and the resurrection, can find peace when they face death. A nurse who spent her career working in hospice once said that her patients without any religious faith tried hardest to hold onto life even as they neared death, while those who were Christians were able to let go and peacefully accept their imminent death.

Christy's Story

That morning, as I gave my speech on hope, I ended with the story of a young woman who was hopeful, even in dying.

The beloved daughter of her physician father and beautiful southern mother, Christy was the only girl born into a family with four older boys. They said they carried her around on a pillow when she was a baby because she was the family princess. She grew up in Asheville, North Carolina; was a high school athlete; attended Davidson College; and then moved to Charlotte, where she eventually became a bank vice president. With a job she loved and abundant friends, whom she called "her posse," Christy had a full life, skiing in Vail in the winter and traveling internationally. Life was good. Then one day, she noticed weakness and muscle twitches in her left arm. The weakness persisted, and soon her parents took her to Johns Hopkins Hospital in Baltimore to confirm a terrifying diagnosis she had already received at the Bowman-Gray School of Medicine in Winston-Salem. There, the doctors had told her that she had ALS. Christy was only thirty-four.

Knowing that she probably had only five years to live, Christy faced her illness with great courage. Of course, she was undone at times. But Christy was a woman of faith, and her Christianity strengthened her in the face of this disastrous diagnosis and enabled her to engage with friends and do something productive with her last few years of life.

Christy and her family created a nonprofit called Race for Research. They traveled, they spoke with experts at prestigious hospitals, and they held fundraisers. And over the years that Christy lived with her illness and growing disability, they joined other groups to raise funds for research that would come to fruition only after Christy's death. Christy's decline was heartbreaking. Her body stiffened, and she could no longer walk or get out of a chair unassisted. Soon, she could not speak, and it was a wrenching day when she was put on a feeding tube. Friends watched Joanna, Christy's mother, lovingly care for her day after day. Christy was always well dressed, and her short hair had a stylish cut. She loved having visitors, and friends came from far and wide. Her four brothers visited often and treated their sister with great love and affection.

At the end of her life, when she was put on a ventilator, Christy was hospitalized, and her friends crowded the waiting room to honor her and to pray. Knowing death was near, Christy, who by this time could only move one eyelid, gave a final message to her family. Working with her mother, who used an alphabet board, she blinked the words, *Tomorrow, I'll be running.* When she died, her father, mother, pastor, and doctor were in the room with her, and Jim, her dad, said Christy was peaceful. "It had been a cloudy morning," said her father, who had been up since five, "but she died peacefully, and as she left us, the sun burst into the room, covering her body."

Tomorrow, I'll be running. From Christy's intense suffering and her deep faith in Christ sprang shimmering hope. She believed, as a Christian whose faith had grown during the five years with ALS, that after death, God would restore her body and give her a new, resurrected body. And she believed that she, the former high school athlete who could only move an eyelid, would soon be restored to full life and vitality.

Christy's courage in the face of her devastating illness, her desire to help others by funding ALS research, and her good cheer with friends and family, as well as her deepening faith in a God who cares—all this was celebrated at the end of her life on earth. The church was packed the day of her memorial service with family and myriad friends—and even President Carter, who had somehow heard about Christy, sent his condolences. Her aunt spoke for many of us when she said that Christy had influenced more people during her thirty-nine years of life than many do who live decades longer.

Never Give Up

I share this unusual story of hope with those of you who may have lost hope in your loved one's recovery, as well as for those struggling with the incapacitating darkness. Don't give up on life. Life is precious even in the midst of a deep and dark clinical depression.

Just ask any individual with cancer who tries drug after drug, fighting to stay alive, even for only a few extra weeks or months. Not only is recovery possible, but it's also likely if the depressive is treated for his illness. This is the time to hang onto hope—when it feels like all hope is gone. This is the time to embrace courage and choose life.

Years ago, a psychotherapist was reeling from a client's suicide. His client had seemed to be doing so much better than she had when she began therapy. She had started an antidepressant, had more energy, spoke of a deepening faith in God, and had made progress in dealing with her difficult family relationships. But unbeknownst to the family or the psychotherapist, she had been hoarding a lethal drug, which she chose to take as her depression lifted and her energy returned. Her family was devastated; her psychotherapist felt as if he had been sucker-punched. Why hadn't he known? What cues had he missed? He had been relieved that his client, who had never indicated she was suicidal, was doing better when all the while she was preparing to take her own life.

One day, weeks after the suicide, the psychotherapist was coming out of a car wash, waiting to claim his car, when he looked across the street at a teeming supermarket where people were shopping on a hot Friday afternoon in preparation for the weekend. The words *They're choosing life* floated into consciousness. He thought these words came from the book of Deuteronomy, but he wasn't sure. As he watched the men, women, and children stream out of the market and load their cars, he realized that they were busy choosing life, no matter what trials or heartaches or difficult situations they also faced at that moment.

Then it came to him that his client had also made a choice—a painful, ultimate, and devastating choice. Heartbreakingly, she lost all hope and chose death. Hers was an irrevocable choice that profoundly affected other lives at the time of her death and for years to come.

Why Suicide?

But why does anyone ever choose to commit suicide? Dr. David Burns says that suicidal patients often believe they have an insoluble problem. He adds,

> You may feel that you are caught in a trap from which there is no exit. This may lead to extreme frustration and even to the urge to kill yourself as the only escape. However, when I confront a depressed patient with respect to precisely what kind of trap he or she is in, and I zero in on the person's "insoluble problem," I invariably find that the patient is deluded. ... Your suicidal thoughts are illogical, distorted, and erroneous. Your twisted thoughts and faulty assumptions, not reality, create your suffering. When you learn to look behind the mirrors, you will see that you are fooling yourself, and your suicidal urge will disappear.[4]

Burns states that he had never seen a "real" problem in a depressed patient that was so "totally insoluble" that suicide was indicated. He believes that all of us have very "real" difficulties that need solutions. But as we cope with our problems, we can experience personal growth and a better mood.[5]

I hope you grasp at this point just how precious life is and how essential it is to hold onto hope, no matter what difficulties life presents. God will help you and the depressive in your life solve those problems that seem insoluble, if only your loved one chooses life.

Choose Life

When the Israelites were preparing to enter the promised land after wandering in the hot, bleak desert for forty years, Moses's words rang out in Deuteronomy 30: "See, I set before you today, life and prosperity, death and destruction. For I command you today to love the LORD your God, to walk in obedience to him, and to keep his commands, decrees and laws; then you will live and increase, and the LORD your God will bless you in the land you are entering to possess."[6] Moses continues,

> This day I call the heavens and the earth as witnesses against you that I have set before you life and death, blessings and curses. Now choose life, so that you and your children may live and that you may love the Lord your God, listen to his voice, and hold fast to him.
>
> For the LORD is your life, and he will give you many years in the land he swore to give to your fathers, Abraham, Isaac and Jacob.[7]

The biblical message is clear. Choose life. Choose precious life, for if we do, untold blessings will follow.

CHAPTER TWELVE

Banishing the Darkness

At times, I feel overwhelmed, and my depression leads me into darkness.
Dorothy Hamill, Olympic gold medalist

He has driven and brought me
into darkness without any light;
surely against me he turns his hand
again and again the whole day long.

Lamentations 3:2 ESV

As we approach the end of our time together, I have saved the best for last. When I was diagnosed with stage-two breast cancer twenty years ago, I believed that to survive, I had to approach this huge health challenge on multiple levels: mind, body, and spirit. It was not enough to just have surgery, take drugs, or engage in psychotherapy. To survive meant going into my soul and purging it of wrongdoing, shame, and bitterness toward others. The same is true in recovering from depression. We have talked about conventional medicine's diagnosis and treatment of this condition, and we have addressed the necessity of forgiveness, but there's a dimension that we have yet to explore in greater depth. In other words, it's time to deal more fully with the heart of the matter. I believe it is in the

spiritual realm that the darkness of depression can be best understood and ultimately banished.

What is this darkness that depressives speak of? They talk as if
they are wandering in a deep, enveloping gloom with no gleam of
light to be seen. It is as if they are lost, alone, isolated, condemned.
And all the while, they hear voices in their heads speaking words of
loathing: "You are worthless." "No one truly cares for your soul."
"You can't do anything right." For the depressive, the darkness per-
meates all of life.

Author John Timmerman describes it thus: "Call it what you
will, the most agonizing fact of the illness is that pall of darkness
laid upon the mind. Life and light seem beyond reach. Something
intervenes: a gray mist of separation, the inability to feel loved
and needed, a feeling of being locked away from everything and
everyone—including God ... Clinically depressed patients cry, 'My
God, why hast thou forsaken me?'—and sometimes add, 'But I
really can't blame you for doing so.' Unworthiness. Forsakenness."[1]

It is a darkness that you, dear reader, cannot fathom unless you
have been clinically depressed yourself. Moreover, you cannot penetrate the darkness your loved one is trapped in, nor can you, try as
you might, lift it. This is not to say that you cannot extend a loving
hand or help in any way you can. But since the darkness invades
soul and spirit, its cure requires something deeply spiritual for its
banishment. It requires the help of someone who has experienced
isolation, pain, and despair greater than we can ever imagine.

It requires Christ and the cross.

On the cross, Christ experienced a terrifying darkness beyond
the pale of human experience when He cried, "My God, my God,

why have you forsaken me?" We cannot begin to imagine what He felt, no matter how many movies we see or books we read. His was a sense of horrific pain and cosmic despair, compounded by the terrible realization of God's absence in those acute moments when He bore the weight of the sins of the world. For a brief time, He experienced intrinsic darkness. But one of the results of this was and is His ability to identify with us when we are lost in our sins and grief.

Drugs Alone Do Not Eradicate the Darkness

Dr. David Allen, a psychiatrist who practices in the Bahamas, understands the spiritual components of depression and says that drugs do not banish the darkness completely. "With drugs we can rearrange chemicals in the brain, but we cannot touch a person's loneliness and isolation," he said. To illustrate his point, he shared the following story:

> One day, an older woman came to see me. She was about seventy. When she entered my office, I felt the room grow dark. And darker. Soon I sensed this tremendous darkness surrounding us. She told me that she had been a Baptist missionary and had of late discovered a tragic family situation that involved [the] two people closest to her, [who were] in a web of betrayal and molestation. She was deeply depressed and said the problem was greater than she was. She knew that no drug would help her. And so she felt she had to kill herself. She had bought a gun. "I gotta die," she said.

As he listened to her story, Allen sensed that her pain was greater than her ability to endure. So he said to her, "You know about the cross of salvation, but do you know about the cross of maintenance?"

"What do you mean?" she asked.

Allen quoted Isaiah 53:4, which says of Christ, "Surely he has borne our griefs and carried our sorrows."[2] He went on to explain to her, "You cannot carry your pain; give this to Christ to carry for you."

Allen said he saw her weekly for about two months, and one day, she appeared in his office carrying a bulging bag with wood protruding from the top. Inside the bag were three roughhewn crosses. Holding them up, she told him that one was for her bedroom at home, one was for his home, and the small one was to be kept in his office "for people who carry pain greater than they can bear." Then Allen knew she had experienced the maintaining power of the cross and that her darkness had begun to lift.

Confession: To Tell the Truth

Another person who understands the power of the cross and church liturgy in helping the depressive is Reverend Claudia Greggs, clergy associate for Christian Formation at Holy Trinity Church in Raleigh, North Carolina. She acknowledges that when people are depressed, they feel a profound sense of separation and isolation: "My guess would be that those who experience depression do feel cut off from everybody and, probably to some degree, from God, if they're believers. That's what the evil one wants to do, to make us think we are cut off from God, and he speaks lies to us, accusing us." As a priest, she has worked with suffering parishioners who have a false sense of who God is or what she calls "God's reality," and it is when they get locked in this "false reality" that the psychological pain is horrendous.

When parishioners come seeking help, Greggs—who says she has learned much from the author Leanne Payne, whose books include *Restoring the Christian Soul, The Healing Presence,* and *The Broken Image*—has them take a piece of paper and draw a line down the middle. On the left side, she asks them to write down things about themselves that they *feel* are true but they know at some level are inaccurate. Then on the other side of the line, she suggests they look at each item and ask God for His perspective, noting that He is "so forgiving and kind." This exercise is to help people see that they are locked into a pattern of thought or a reality that is not true. "It is their own false reality because God says we are precious, redeemed by the blood of His Son, Jesus," states Greggs.

Then Greggs leads the parishioner through Confession, the ancient liturgy that she says isn't purely cognitive but speaks to both heart and mind. "Confession," says Greggs, "simply means to tell the truth." It is telling the sometimes-hidden truth, articulating the hurts, sins, and powerful darkness lodged in the secret places of the heart. In the process of confession, Greggs has the parishioner close his eyes and imagine Jesus on the cross. And if he has difficulty doing this, she has a reproduction of Matthias Grunewald's sixteenth-century painting *The Small Crucifixion,* a study done by the painter in preparation for the Isenheim Altarpiece, in her office.

In this work of art, the greatest German Renaissance artist painted a tortured, twisted Christ with closed eyes and a body covered with blood, wounds, splinters, and green pustules. Why green pustules? The monastery-hospital that commissioned the altarpiece specialized in caring for those suffering from the plague as well as skin diseases, such as ergotism, a result of eating toxic rye. When the diseased patients looked at the painting of Christ in the monastery chapel and saw that his body had plague-like sores just like theirs, they knew he truly carried their diseases and shared in their painful afflictions.[3]

As the individual imagines Christ on the cross, Greggs suggests that he name not only his sins but the sins of others against him. She adds, "Often we sin out of being sinned against. Ours is a grievous reaction to sin. But all sin is weighty, and we cannot bear it. And the person who is depressed can no longer hold up under the weight of sin. We have to name and lay our sins on Him who is the sin-bearer, Christ. If we don't confess, the poison stays with us." Greggs adds, "It's not enough to understand. We have to confess, to tell the truth."

In explaining the act of laying our sins on the sin-bearer, Greggs mentions Leviticus 16 and the Day of Atonement. On that particular day in Jewish history, the priest went into the Holy of Holies and sacrificed a bull as a sin offering for himself and his house. Then a ram was brought to him as a burnt offering, as well as two goats. One goat was to be sacrificed for the sins of Israel, and the other was chosen to bear the sins of Israel into the wilderness. After sacrificing the first goat, Aaron, the high priest, laid his hands on the head of the other goat, confessing all the sins Israel had committed the preceding year. This goat, called a scapegoat, was then led out into the wilderness to wander and die.

"Christ is our scapegoat and sin-bearer," says Greggs. She adds that in John 19:30, as Christ breathes his last breath, he utters the words, "It is finished." Greggs explains, "That means that our sins are paid for, and we can stop trying to pay for them ourselves." She also believes in the power of forgiveness. "If we can't forgive, then we don't understand how much we have been forgiven. If we have received God's forgiveness, that's the fuel we need to forgive."

Greggs follows Confession with Absolution or a blessing as the confessor departs. She reminds him that he is forgiven, that he is God's beloved son, and that now is the time to receive God's blessing and go in peace.

Will Confession bring healing and dispel the darkness? Greggs notes that parishioners have told her that Confession is "incredibly powerful." As for dispelling the darkness, she believes it can be a significant part of the journey out of darkness into the healing power of the light of God's love and acceptance.

A Day of Atonement

At this point, you may be saying, "But neither I nor the depressed loved one in my life attend a church that offers a time of private confession with a priest or minister." Then I would suggest that you and your loved one take a day and go separately to a private, quiet, and beautiful place and have your own time of confession before God. Call this day your own personal day of atonement. Take your journal and a Bible and sit before the Lord. Write down all your anger, bitterness, resentment, and hatred toward others. Add any sin that you deeply regret or that brings you shame. The Scottish preacher and writer George MacDonald has this to say about shame:

We may trust God with our past as heartily as with our future. It will not hurt us so long as we do not try to hide things, so long as we are ready to bow our heads in hearty shame where it is fit we should be ashamed. For to be ashamed is a holy and blessed thing. Shame is a thing to shame only those who want to appear, not those who want to be. Shame is to shame those who want to pass their examination, not those who would get into the heart of things. ... To be humbly ashamed is to be plunged in the cleansing bath of truth.[4]

Admit not only that you have been wronged but that you have wronged others. Write down all that comes to mind. Then, one by one, confess these sins to God and ask for forgiveness. And when you have finished, destroy the paper and leave the place in peace, believing that you have been heard and forgiven. And in the coming days, see if the darkness begins to lift.

Cover Your Life with Prayer

Even if you and the depressive in your life are not people who pray often, now is the time to learn about the enormous value of prayer—of praying about your life, your every need, your sorrows, your longings. Now is the time to simply pray. And if you can, pray *with* the depressed person in your life; if she isn't willing, you can pray for her and her inner healing. Those of us who have witnessed the intervention of God in our lives because of prayer are committed to praying about everything. Once you have seen God heal broken or estranged relationships or extend the life of someone who has cancer far beyond what the doctors decreed, then you know that He hears and answers prayer.

The power of prayer became intensely real to me twenty years ago when I was diagnosed with breast cancer. I was terrified and believed I might die. Consequently, I went to healing services whenever I could and received sweet, believing, intercessory prayers. I have just celebrated twenty years of being cancer-free. But it was not too long after the discovery of cancer that I learned I also had serious heart disease. I was shocked when I had a heart attack! Again, Don and I prayed earnestly that God would spare my life. So far, He has.

I could not live without the power of prayer. For me, prayer is like breathing. I breathe out my prayers day and night. I breathe in the assurance of God's love. Prayer has helped save my life, and it keeps me out of the depression pit.

John Rice, a retired Anglican priest who has himself suffered from clinical depression, often prays for the depressives who come to his workshops on prayer and healing. When this warm-hearted priest prays aloud, his hands lightly touching the petitioner's shoulders, he asks God to lift the darkness. He says it is rare for the depressive not to experience some relief after healing prayer. As noted in Chapter Ten, forgiveness is critical in the life of the depressive. Rice adds that forgiveness "is the key to healing—it unlocks the door" and begins to banish the darkness. Rice says that depression and its accompanying darkness rob us of joy, "yet Jesus wants us to have joy because we are God's beloved sons and daughters."

Go toward the Light

Our journey together has come to an end, and I hope you not only have learned helpful concepts but also have been encouraged. We have looked at conventional treatments for depression and how depression differs between the sexes. We have also looked at who gets depressed and why. Finally, we have gone beyond mind and body to encounter the soul and the cross as a way of coming out of the darkness and moving into the light of God's love for us.

Scripture tells us that God is light and that if we walk in the light, we have fellowship not only with Him but with each other. We should thus valiantly move toward the light until we feel its warmth surround and embrace our whole being. What sufferer does not want to be free? What person does not want the one he loves to recover from depression and experience freedom, joy, and love again? Confession, prayer, forgiveness, and a day of atonement—all these ancient spiritual disciplines enable us to begin our journey toward the light until we can echo Samuel, who says, "You, Lord, are my lamp; the Lord turns my darkness into light."[5]

Let us begin.

Notes

Preface

1 "Depression," Assessment Psychology Online, last modified September 13, 2006, www.assessmentpsychology.com/depression.htm.

2 Sally C. Curtin, Margaret Warner, and Holly Hedegaard, "Increase in Suicide in the United States, 1999–2014," Centers for Disease Control and Prevention, last modified April 22, 2016, www.cdc.gov/nchs/products/databriefs/db241.htm.

Chapter Two

1 "J. K. Rowling, Harry Potter and Depression," *HBC Protocols*, last modified February 28, 2008, http://talentdevelop.com/articles/JKRHPAD.html.

2 "J. K. Rowling," *HBC Protocols.*

3 "J. K. Rowling," *HBC Protocols.*

4 Boris Johnson, *The Churchill Factor: How One Man Made History* (New York: Riverhead Books, 2014), 70.

5 Ceci Connolly, "Tipper Gore Details Depression Treatment," *Washington Post*, May 8, 1999, www.washingtonpost.com/wp-srv/politics/campaigns/wh2000/stories/tipper050899.htm.

6 Psalm 143:3–4, 7 NLT.

7 Jonah 4:3 ESV.

8   Jonah 4:4 and Jonah 4:9.

9   Richard O'Connor, *Undoing Depression: What Therapy Doesn't Teach You* (New York: Berkley Books,1997), 142.

10   O'Connor, *Undoing Depression*, 72.

11   Douglas F. Levinson and Walter E. Nichols, "Major Depression and Genetics," Stanford School of Medicine, accessed March 23, 2017, http://depressiongenetics.stanford.edu/mddandgenes.html.

12   American Psychiatric Association (APA), *Diagnostic and Statistical Manual of Mental Disorders (DSM-5) Fifth Edition* (Arlington, VA: American Psychiatric Association, 2013), 155.

13   APA, *DSM-5*, 161.

14   APA, *DSM-5*, 170.

15   APA, *DSM-5*, 168.

16   APA, *DSM-5*, 156–57.

17   APA, *DSM-5*, 171–72.

18   APA, *DSM-5*, 178.

19   APA, *DSM-5*, 178.

20   Falk W. Lohoff, "Overview of the Genetics of Major Depressive Disorder," *Current Psychiatry Reports* 12, no. 6 (December 2010): 539–46, doi: 10.1007/s11920-010-0150-6.

21   Erica L. Weiss, James G. Longhurst, and Carolyn M. Mazure, "Childhood Sexual Abuse as a Risk Factor for Depression in Women: Psychosocial and Neurobiological Correlates," *American Journal of Psychiatry* 156, no. 6 (June 1999): 816–18, doi: 10.1176/ajp.156.6.816.

22   John Bowlby, *Attachment and Loss*, vol. 3, *Loss: Sadness and Depression* (London: Basic Books, 1980), 248.

23   William Styron, *Darkness Visible: A Memoir of Madness* (New York: Random House, 1990), 56.

24   Styron, *Darkness Visible*, 79.

25   APA, *DSM-5*, 167.

26   Sally C. Curtin, Margaret Warner, and Holly Hedegaard, "Increase in Suicide in the United States, 1999–2014," Centers for Disease Control and Prevention, last modified April 22, 2016, www.cdc.gov/nchs/products/databriefs/db241.htm.

Chapter Three

1   Mayo Clinic Staff, "Male Depression: Understanding the Issues," MayoClinic.org, last modified May 17, 2016, www.mayoclinic.org/diseases-conditions/depression/in-depth/male-depression/art-20046216.

2   Mayo Clinic Staff, "Male Depression."

3   Sally C. Curtin, Margaret Warner, and Holly Hedegaard, "Increase in Suicide in the United States, 1999–2014," Centers for Disease Control and Prevention, last modified April 22, 2016, www.cdc.gov/nchs/products/databriefs/db241.htm.

4   Walker Percy, *The Second Coming* (New York: Washington Square Press, 1980), 144.

Chapter Four

1   "Depression in Women," PsychGuides.com, accessed March 22, 2017, www.psychguides.com/guides/depression -in-women.

2   Christa Andrews-Fike, "A Review of Postpartum Depression," *Primary Care Companion to the Journal of Clinical Psychiatry* 1, no. 1 (February 1999): 9–14.

3   Brooke Shields, "War of Words," *New York Times*, July 1, 2005.

4   Shields, "War of Words."

5   Pam Belluck, "After a Baby, an Unraveling: A Case Study in Maternal Mental Illness," *New York Times*, June 16, 2014, www.nytimes.com/2014/06/17/health/maternal-mental -illness-can-arrive-months-after-baby.html.

6   Belluck, "After a Baby."

Chapter Five

1   Susanna Schrobsdorff, "Teen Depression and Anxiety: Why the Kids Are Not Alright," *Time*, November 7, 2016, 47.

2   Schrobsdorff, "Teen Depression and Anxiety," 46.

3   Schrobsdorff, "Teen Depression and Anxiety," 47.

4   Schrobsdorff, "Teen Depression and Anxiety," 47.

5   Sherry Turkle, *Alone Together: Why We Expect More from Technology and Less from Each Other* (New York: Basic Books, 2011), 1.

6   Mayo Clinic Staff, "Teen Suicide: What Parents Need to Know," MayoClinic.org, last modified April 19, 2016,

www.mayoclinic.org/healthy-lifestyle/tween-and-teen health/in-depth/teen-suicide/art-200443087pg=2.

7   Sally C. Curtin, Margaret Warner, and Holly Hedegaard, "Increase in Suicide in the United States, 1999–2014," Centers for Disease Control and Prevention, last modified April 22, 2016, www.cdc.gov/nchs/products/databriefs/ db241.htm.

8   Centers for Disease Control and Prevention, "Youth Risk Behavior Surveillance—United States, 2015," *Morbidity and Mortality Weekly Report: Surveillance Summaries* 65, no. 6 (June 10, 2016).

9   Hanna Rosin, "The Silicon Valley Suicides," *Atlantic*, September 2015, 64.

10   Rosin, "Silicon Valley Suicides," 64.

11   "Henry M. Gunn High School: 1 More Suicide Preventable," YouTube video, 3:25, posted by "martha cabot," November 4, 2014, www.youtube.com/watch?v=9LLnY _JBAAg.

12   Rosin, "Silicon Valley Suicides," 70.

13   Rosin, "Silicon Valley Suicides," 68–69.

14   Rosin, "Silicon Valley Suicides," 68.

15   Schrobsdorff, "Teen Depression and Anxiety," 48.

16   Sue Shellenbarger, "Teenage Girls: An Expert Guide," *Wall Street Journal*, April 12, 2017, A8–9.

17   Rosin, "Silicon Valley Suicides," 66.

Chapter Six

1   John Bowlby, *Attachment and Loss*, vol. 1, *Attachment*, 2nd. ed. (New York: Basic Books, 1982), 177.

2   John Bowlby, *A Secure Base: Parent-Child Attachment and Healthy Human Development* (New York: Basic Books, 1988), 120–21.

3   Bowlby, *Secure Base*, 124.

4   Bowlby, *Secure Base*, 124.

5   Bowlby, *Secure Base*, 124.

6   Bowlby, *Secure Base*, 125.

7   Bowlby, *Secure Base*, 125–26.

8   John Bowlby, *Attachment and Loss*, vol. 3, *Loss: Sadness and Depression* (London: Basic Books, 1980), 247.

9   Bowlby, *Attachment and Loss*, 247.

10 John Bowlby, address given at a workshop at the American Psychiatric Association (APA) convention in Washington, DC, 1986.

11 Boris Johnson, *The Churchill Factor: How One Man Made History* (New York: Riverhead Books, 2014), 40–41.

12 Johnson, *Churchill Factor*, 40–41.

13 Johnson, *Churchill Factor*, 109.

14 Johnson, *Churchill Factor*, 110.

15 Johnson, *Churchill Factor*, 111.

16 Johnson, *Churchill Factor*, 126.

Chapter Seven

1   David D. Burns, *Feeling Good: The New Mood Therapy*, rev. ed. (1980; repr., New York: HarperCollins, 2008), xix.

2   Burns, *Feeling Good*, xix.

3   Burns, *Feeling Good*, 29.

4   Burns, *Feeling Good*, 28.

5   Burns, *Feeling Good*, 29.

6   Burns, *Feeling Good*, 31.

7   Burns, *Feeling Good*, 32.

8   Burns, *Feeling Good*, 42–43.

Chapter Eight

1   Sebastian Junger, *Tribe: On Homecoming and Belonging* (New York: Twelve, 2016), xvii.

2   Junger, *Tribe*, 3.

3   Karl Vick, "Sebastian Junger Says PTSD Is Our Fault," *Time*, June 27, 2016, 60.

4   Junger, *Tribe*, 21.

5   Junger, *Tribe*, 93.

6   Harville Hendrix, *Getting the Love You Want: A Guide for Couples* (New York: Henry Holt, 1988), 93.

7   Hendrix, *Getting the Love*, 93.

8   David D. Burns, *Feeling Good: The New Mood Therapy*, rev. ed. (1980; repr., New York: HarperCollins, 2008), 42–43.

9   Dietrich Bonhoeffer, *Life Together: The Classic Exploration of Christian Community* (New York: Harper & Brothers, 1954), 19.

10 Bonhoeffer, *Life Together*, 19.

11 Bonhoeffer, *Life Together*, 20.

12 Bonhoeffer, *Life Together*, 21.

Chapter Nine

1   Donald O. Rudin and Clara Felix, *Omega 3 Oils: A Practical Guide* (Garden City Park, NY: Avery, 1996), 15.

2   Brenda Hunter, *Staying Alive: Life-Changing Strategies for Surviving Cancer* (Colorado Springs, CO: Water Brook Press, 2004), 62.

3   "Anti-inflammatory Diet & Pyramid," Weil Lifestyle, accessed March 23, 2017, www.drweil.com/diet-nutrition/anti-inflammatory-diet-pyramid/.

4   Joseph R. Hibbein, "Fish Consumption and Major Depression," *Lancet* 351, no. 9110 (April 18, 1998): 1213, doi: 10.1016/S0140-6736(05)79168-6.

5   Dr. Andrew Weil's Daily Health Tips, "5 Reasons You Shouldn't Eat Farmed Fish," Weil Lifestyle, August 16, 2014, www.drweilblog.com/home/2014/8/16/5-reasons-you-shouldnt-eat-farmed-fish.html.

6   Marylou Tousignant, "50 Years Later, These Girls Are Still in the Game," *Washington Post*, June 13, 1999, www.washingtonpost.com/archive/local/1999/06/13/50-years-later-these-girls-are-still-in-the-game/586325f6-9c56-4594-b26d-0fde8a1002f4/.

7   Dante Alighieri, *The Inferno*, in *The Divine Comedy*, trans. John Ciardi (New York: W. W. Norton, 1977), Canto I, 4.

8   Langston Hughes, *The Collected Poems of Langston Hughes*, ed. Arnold Rampersad (New York: Vintage Books, 1994), 32.

Chapter Ten

1 Frederic Luskin, *Forgive for Good: A Proven Prescription for Health and Happiness*, rev. ed. (New York: HarperOne, 2003), vii–viii.

2 Luskin, *Forgive for Good*, viii.

3 Matthew 18:35 ESV.

4 George MacDonald, *George MacDonald Anthology*, ed. C. S. Lewis (London: Geoffrey Bles, 1970), 26–27.

5 C. S. Lewis, *Letters to an American Lady*, ed. Clyde S. Kilby (London: Hodder & Stoughton, 1969), 117.

Chapter Eleven

1 Romans 4.

2 Romans 5:3–4.

3 Hebrews 6:18–19.

4 David D. Burns, *Feeling Good: The New Mood Therapy*, rev. ed. (1980; repr., New York: HarperCollins, 1999), 405.

5 Burns, *Feeling Good*, 405.

6 Deuteronomy 30:15–16.

7 Deuteronomy 30:19–20.

Chapter Twelve

1 John H. Timmerman, "Shedding Light on the Darkness of Depression," *Christian Century*, March 2, 1988, www.religion-online.org/showarticle.asp?title=939.

2 ESV.

3   "The Isenhelm Altarpiece (c. 1515)," visual-arts-cork.com, accessed March 23, 2017, www.visual-arts-cork.com/ famous-paintings/isenheim-altarpiece.htm.

4   George MacDonald, *George MacDonald Anthology*, ed. C. S. Lewis (London: Geoffrey Bles, 1946), 95.

5   2 Samuel 22:29.

NEWLIFE

Help in Life's Hardest Places

Talking about the things no one else will, to bring healing to those who've lost hope

"*I have been living with my secrets* for 30 plus years while failing time and again to stop and all the while them getting worse. For the first time I have learned more about why it is happening, developing an action plan to change, and creating a network of support."

— Jack
Intensive Workshop attendee

NEW LIFE MINISTRIES EXISTS
TO GO INTO LIFE'S HARDEST PLACES

With you.

800-HELP-4-ME
NewLife.com

When you or someone you love is in crisis, you need a trusted friend to walk alongside you—a helper who's been there and understands, but who also has the training and skill to offer practical help.

New Life Ministries, founded by Steve Arterburn, exists to go into life's hardest places with you.

For over 30 years, we've provided expert answers to people just like you on our call-in radio show, *New Life Live!* We also offer a host of other resources, Intensive Workshops, and referrals to a carefully selected network of counselors.

Visit NewLife.com today to see how we can help, or call 800-HELP-4-ME. We want to hear from you!

At David C Cook, we equip the local church around the corner and around the globe to make disciples. Come see how we are working together—go to **www.davidccook.com**. Thank you!

transforming lives together